Public Policy and Local Crises

STUDIES IN POLITICS, SECURITY AND SOCIETY

Edited by Stanisław Sulowski
Faculty of Political Science and International Studies
University of Warsaw

VOLUME 65

Robert Geisler and Tomasz Pawłuszko (eds.)

Public Policy and Local Crises

Lessons from Poland and Central Europe

PETER LANG
Berlin · Bruxelles · Chennai · Lausanne · New York · Oxford

Bibliographic Information published by the Deutsche Nationalbibliothek
The Deutsche Nationalbibliothek lists this publication in the Deutsche Nationalbibliografie; detailed bibliographic data is available online at http://dnb.d-nb.de.

Library of Congress Cataloging-in-Publication Data
LCCN number 2025024115

The cover image courtesy of Benjamin Ben Chaim.

The publication is published thanks to the support of the University of Opole.

ISSN 2199-028X
ISBN 978-3-631-93744-0 (Print)
ISBN 978-3-631-93745-7 (E-PDF)
ISBN 978-3-631-94133-1 (E-PUB)
DOI 10.3726/b23090

Published by Peter Lang GmbH, Berlin (Germany)

info@peterlang.com

This publication has been peer reviewed.

www.peterlang.com

Contents

Introduction: Public Policy and Local Crises

Robert Geisler, Tomasz Pawłuszko[1]

One of the first tasks of public policies was to counteract threats to the government. The first ministries established concerned the state treasury, war, diplomacy and internal security. In the nineteenth century, two parallel processes occurred that increased the role of the modern state. The first process was economic in nature. Industrialization led to the migration of people to cities and rapid economic development. Many areas of the economy emerged that had to be taxed and regulated. Secondly, the development of constitutionalism and the democratization of the political systems of European states led to the expansion of the modern legal infrastructure. The effect of these processes was the expansion of regulations in every area of social life.

For most of the twentieth century, the population of Europe lived in the shadow of two world wars and the Cold War. Fears of another world war led to the establishment of numerous systems of civil protection. Despite the risks associated with the potential escalation of the conflict between the USA and the USSR, long-term economic development and technological progress allowed for the growth of the importance of science, engineering and new technologies. These processes were followed by the social sciences, which tried to understand the modern human condition.

During the Cold War, many intellectual trends influenced the way social threats were constructed. These included, among others, the systemic school and new institutionalism, which emphasized the key role of the context of social actions[2]. Regulations of the public sphere began to concern the quality

---

1 Robert Geisler, University of Opole, Associate Professor, The Chair of the Governance and Public Policy Department. https://orcid.org/0000-0002-0218-980X; Tomasz Pawłuszko - University of Opole, Assistant Professor, Department of Governance and Public Policy. https://orcid.org/0000-0002-5572-3199

2 J. G. March, J. P. Olsen, "The New Institutionalism: Organizational Factors in Political Life", *The American Political Science Review*, Vol. 78, No. 3 (Sep., 1984), pp. 734–749. DOI: https://doi.org/10.2307/1961840

of life of the population. The importance of economic and educational policies increased. Numerous new security services and systems were created[3].

At the end of the twentieth century, concepts such as VUCA, risk and globalization appeared, which are still explored today. Security sciences were also created, which deal with the study of threats and methods of counteracting them. The issue of non-military security gained enormous importance. Barry Buzan pointed out that, in addition to the problem of survival, values such as sovereignty, prosperity, justice, identity, and sustainable development are important for public security[4]. The dynamic development of the media has also shown us the growing role of communication.

The first decades of the 21st century made political elites aware of the scale of threats such as terrorism, internationalized civil wars, migration, pandemics, and piracy. Climate change, in turn, led to an increased demand for understanding natural disasters and catastrophes. The universality of perceived threats and the rapid ability to communicate have increased the pressure for more effective political actions. Public policies are today an important tool for ensuring security and preventing crises.

This book is devoted to the various responses of state structures to non-military threats. The book consists of several case studies, the development of which has theoretical, educational, and practical value for the international reader. The publication is part of the current trend of contemporary public policy research, with particular emphasis on the issue of crisis management. In the following summary, we present the key concepts that influenced the authors of the individual chapters.

Risk analysis

The scientific study of threats led to the development of security sciences[5]. The possibilities of determining future threats are called risk. Therefore, one of the key research areas of these sciences is risk analysis. The concept of risk has a

---

3 M. Vedby Rasmussen, *Risk and Security*, in: *Oxford Research Encyclopedia of International Studies*, Oxford University Press, Oxford – New York 2017. DOI: https://doi.org/10.1093/acrefore/9780190846626.013.290

4 B. Buzan, O. Waever, J. de Wilde, *Security. A New Framework for Analysis*, Lynne Rienner Publishers, Boulder – London 1998, pp. 10–28.

5 C. L. Smith, J. Brooks, *Security Science: The Theory and Practice of Security*, Butterworth-Heinemann, Waldham – Oxford 2013, pp. 23–78.

long history and is associated with the process of assessing threats[6]. This issue is crucial for managing the security of both the public and private spheres.

The first comprehensive risk analyses in the assessment of public policies were conducted in the 1970s. Private companies tried to understand political behaviors that affect the allocation of money in the economy and thus tried to assess long-term conditions for conducting business[7]. Understanding the logic of decision-makers' functioning was of key importance. Risk analysis was associated with comparative research, behavioral analysis and research on information. In their cross-sectional work, V. Covello, J. Menkes and J. Nehnevajsa outlined several prospective areas of risk management research[8]. The issue that raised the greatest doubt was the problem of uncertainty. In the late 1990s, Sheila Jasanoff defined several risk models in the perception of public policies[9].

Table 1: Model of risk perception for public policy

Model	Epistemology	Location of authority	Political prescriptions	
			Style	Mechanism
Realist	Realist	Expert communities	Managerial	Expert advice
Constructivist	Constructivist	Interest groups	Pluralist	Public participation
Discursive	Constructivist	Professional discourses	Critical	Social movement

S. Jasanoff, The political science of risk perception, *Reliability Engineering and System Safety*, vol. 59, 1998, p. 94.

6 T. Aven, "The risk concept—historical and recent development trends", *Reliability, Engineering and System Safety*, vol. 99 (2012), pp. 33–44. DOI: https://doi.org/10.1016/j.ress.2011.11.006

7 S. J. Kobrin, "Political Risk: A Review and Reconsideration", *Journal of International Business Studies*, Vol. 10, No. 1 (Spring - Summer, 1979), pp. 67–80. DOI: https://doi.org/10.1057/palgrave.jibs.8490631

8 V. T. Covello, J. Menkes, J. Nehnevajsa, "Risk Analysis, Philosophy, and the Social and Behavioral Sciences: Reflections on the Scope of Risk Analysis Research", *Risk Analysis*, Vol. 2, no. 2, 1982, pp. 53–58. DOI: https://doi.org/10.1111/j.1539-6924.1982.tb01366.x

9 S. Jasanoff, "The political science of risk perception", *Reliability Engineering and System Safety*, vol. 59, 1998, pp. 91–99. DOI: https://doi.org/10.1016/S0951-8320(97)00129-4

The above list indicates the significant role of elites in the process of risk recognition. These findings are consistent with contemporary political science theory, which points to three main dimensions of governance: decision-making, agenda-setting and preference-shaping. Contemporary explanations of public policies include such objects as decision-makers, their agenda and relations with the political environment[10]. Risk analysis has become important for optimistic liberal societies, which strive to secure success through political programming.

In subsequent years, the concept of "risk society" presented by the German sociologist Ulrich Beck had a major influence on social sciences[11]. Further studies have shown the diversity of sources of risk resulting from threats. Modern researchers divide threats into natural (geological, climatic, environmental), technical (failures, catastrophes, fires) and anthropogenic (military threats, terrorism, epidemics, social issues, etc.)[12].

To summarize this argument, risk management has become a complex interdisciplinary scientific process, in which experts from various fields try to predict risks and prevent crises[13]. This process has become particularly important in a situation of growing non-military threats. Contemporary research is also related to concepts such as resilience, uncertainty, complexity, and quality of governance. All these issues are connected by the ever-important problem of the effectiveness of anti-crisis institutions.

---

10 C. Hay, *Political Analysis. A Critical Introduction*, Palgrave Macmillan, London & New York 2002, pp. 172–180.

11 U. Beck, *Risk Society. Towards a New Modernity*, Sage Publications, London – Newbury Park – New Delhi 1992 (the book was originally published in Germany in 1986, by the Suhrkamp Verlag)

12 H. Wyrębek, "National Security Challenges and Threats", *Wiedza Obronna*, 2022, Vol. 279 No. 2, pp. 109–122. DOI: https://doi.org/10.34752/2022-e279

13 B. Wiśniewski, B. Kaczmarczyk, "Opportunity, Challenge, Risk and Threat - Review of Definitions and Relations", *Internal Security*, vol. 9, no. 2, 2017, pp. 23–32. http://dx.doi.org/10.5604/01.3001.0012.1699 On forecasting: T. Aleksandrowicz, "Forecasting Threats to State Security in Theory and in Practice. Toolbox for the Analyst", *Internal Security*, Vol. 15, No. 1, 2023, pp. 7–21. DOI: http://dx.doi.org/10.5604/01.3001.0053.9579

VUCA

The VUCA world emerged in the literature of management studies at the end of 20th century. Dominated by the notions such as variability, uncertainty, complexity and ambiguity, it presents mostly the reality of economy as constantly changing, unpredictable and deprived of full market information where managers, entrepreneurs and employees function by performing their daily activities. Additionally, not only business and economy were involved in this model. It extended into all areas of life as political, cultural and social[14]. All provided processes point to a new context of governance, organizations, entrepreneurship, as well as every-day living. The new type of features started to be emphasised in the new model, including flexibility, the search for new products and services, the creation of innovative products, the implementation of these innovative solutions for individual customers (customisation), the use of knowledge and information to implement business ventures, the use of social networks to implement business projects, and the use of Internet technology to pursue business[15].

It serves as a powerful lens for understanding the far-reaching effects of political and natural disasters. Volatility manifests in the sudden escalation of conflicts and climate-induced disasters, displacing millions and reshaping entire regions. Uncertainty prevails as governments struggle to predict or manage crises effectively, leaving vulnerable populations to navigate an unpredictable landscape of survival. Whether it is the unforeseen eruption of civil unrest or the rapid intensification of storms and floods, the accelerating pace of these crises underscores the volatile nature of our times. The complexity defines the set of contemporary crises amplified by their interdependent nature, where political instability and natural disasters often feed into one another. Ambiguity arises from the overlapping responsibilities of local, national, and international bodies, creating confusion in both preventive measures and emergency responses[16].

---

14 L. Ortega (ed.) *Managing in a VUCA World* (Volatility, Uncertainty, Complexity and Ambiguity). Murphy & Moore Publishing, 2023.

15 N. Bennett & G. J. Lemoine, *What VUCA Really Means for You*. Harvard Business Review, 2014.

16 C. C. Millar, J. M., Groth, J. F. Mahon, "Management Innovation in a VUCA World: Challenges and Recommendations", *California Management Review*, 61 (1), 2018, pp. 5–14. DOI: https://doi.org/10.1177/0008125618805111

Flood

Floods are among the most frequent and devastating natural disasters, which have far-reaching consequences not only for the environment but also for societies. While the hydrological and geomorphological aspects of floods are well described in the scientific literature[17], the social impacts of these disasters require broader and deeper reflection and interdisciplinary analyses. Flooding, as a social disaster, can reveal weaknesses in the institutional system, the public management model, or the adaptation mechanisms of communities of local communities and the related actions of local authorities.

Contemporary research on disasters emphasises that their impacts are largely determined by social factors such as demographic structure, level of economic development, spatial policies or disaster management systems crisis management[18]. The phenomenon of flooding is not limited to material losses. Research points to long-term psychosocial effects, such as post-traumatic stress, weakened social ties, or changes in perceptions of safety. Reconstruction after a flood is not only an emergency management process of local authorities but also a broad social process that requires support psychological support and the rebuilding of social capital[19].

The concept of social resilience, which encompasses a community's ability to prepare for, respond to and recover from a hazard, is playing an increasingly important role in the disaster management literature. Social capital, which has been analysed by researchers for nearly forty years, plays a key role in this, as it determines the capacity for cooperation, self-organisation and effective crisis management. While previous analyses of social capital have been conducted in the context of regional development, economic growth, or building the social fabric, such as civil society, it has found a new research challenge in relation to natural disasters.

---

17 T. Kałuża, M. Hämmerling, P. Zawadzki, W. Czekała, R. Kasperek, M. Sojka, M. Mokwa, M. Ptak, A. Szkudlarek, M. Czechlowski, "The hydropower sector in Poland: Historical development and current status", *Renewable and Sustainable Energy Reviews*. Vol. 158, April, 2022. DOI: 10.1016/j.rser.2022.11215

18 D. E. Alexander, "Resilience and disaster risk reduction: an etymological journey", *Nat. Hazards Earth Syst. Sci.*, 13, 2013, pp. 2707–2716. https://doi.org/10.5194/nhess-13-2707-2013

19 D. P. Aldrich, *Building Resilience Social Capital in Post-Disaster Recovery*, University of Chicago Press, Chicago 2012. DOI: https://doi.org/10.7208/chicago/9780226012896.001.0001

Public policies

Public policies in relation to natural disasters are an extremely complex field that requires consideration of both preventive and reactive factors. The scientific literature based on previous research results offers a broad spectrum of approaches to the issue, considering both theories of disaster management and the practical aspects of public policies that shape the responses of nation-states with their local, regional and national institutions, as well as the international organisations to disasters. Natural disaster-related public policies cover a wide range of issues, from prevention to preparedness to emergency management, crisis management, approaches to prevention, state response to the crises and post-disaster infrastructure reconstruction. Contemporary research on these issues takes into account technical, as well as social, political and economic aspects. All of these are directly relevant to the decisions of governments, local authorities and different kinds of organisations (mostly NGO's).

From the perspective of political science and sociology, natural disasters are not only phenomena with natural dimensions but also moments that reveal weaknesses in social structures, political systems and crisis management mechanisms. Understanding how disasters shape political and social responses is crucial for developing effective prevention and relief strategies. The analysis of the impact of such events on long-term social development would also be a very interesting perspective for research.

In the sociology of disasters, researchers pay attention to the roles that factors such as power, social inequality, culture, social norms and solidarity play in emergencies. Political science, on the other hand, examines how power structures, public policies, particularisms of interest and ideologies shape responses to natural crises. The analysis of crisis management policies, which can have a decisive impact on the effectiveness of post-disaster responses, is also an important issue.

Communication

Communication in crisis management during natural disasters is one of the fundamental issues for shaping public policies. Communication in the crises is the process of exchanging information between local/regional authorities and the community in emergency situations to minimize losses, protect the health and lives of residents and maintain public order. Effective communication should be fast, reliable and adapted to dynamically changing crisis conditions[20].

In the case of flooding, the transmission of threat information, guidance on preventive measures, evacuation planning, and information about available support services are all critical. Lack of adequate communication can lead to misinformation, panic or ignoring warnings, increasing the risk to the population. Communication should be a key element of emergency management. Municipal authorities should follow proven communication models, use a variety of information channels and eliminate barriers to information access. Adopting a multi-channel strategy and effectively monitoring the community's response can significantly improve the effectiveness of information efforts, increasing the safety of residents and minimising the impact of the disaster[21].

The following best practices of effective emergency communication during floods could be applied, like transparency and reliability, which means timely, accurate and in line with reality information, speed of response, multichannel transmission combining different methods of communication to increase the reach of information, monitoring and message adaptation, and community engagement[22].

* * *

The structure of the book is as follows. In the next chapter, Tomasz Pawłuszko analyzes civil protection policies in Central Europe after the escalation of the Russian-Ukrainian War. The chapter concerns the problems in the development of public policies in Central Europe in response to the Russian-Ukrainian war. Due to mass migrations and increased security

---

[20] E. Rolarson, L. J. Bracken, R. J. Hardy, A. R. G. Large, "Rethinking Flood Risk Communication", *Natural hazards*, Vol 92, pp 1665 – 1686, March 2018. DOI: https://doi.org/10.1007/s11069-018-3273-4

[21] E. Intrieri, J. Dotta, K. Fontanelli, Ch. Bianchini, F. Bardi, F. Campatelli, N. Casagli, "Operational Framework for Flood Risk Communicatio", *International Journal of Disaster Risk Reduction*. Vol. 46, June 2020. DOI: https://doi.org/10.1016/j.ijdrr.2020.101510

[22] C. A. Lin, "Participatory Flood Risk Management and Environmental Sustainability: The Role of Communication Engagement, Severity Beliefs, Mitigation Barriers and Social Efficacy", *Sustainability*, 17, 2844 2025. DOI: https://doi.org/10.3390/su17072844

risks, the countries of the region faced the challenge of modernizing civil protection structures. The author's aim is to answer the questions (1) what changes in civil protection policies were introduced and (2) whether the adaptations led to the emergence of a new model of crisis management.

In the next chapter, Robert Geisler examines the adaptation processes of Ukrainian migrants in Germany. After analyzing qualitative and statistical data, the author concludes that the German labour market has numerous difficulties in absorbing new workers and proposes several solutions to this problem.

In the next chapter, Bartosz Maziarz analyzes cooperation of emergency services in the face of flood threats. Using the Opolskie Voivodeship as a case study, this chapter demonstrates how effective collaboration among these services can significantly mitigate the impacts of natural disasters and protect the lives and properties of citizens.

The next chapter was written by Rafał Kochańczyk. The author analyzes the crucial role of the Polish Police in crisis management during floods in the Opole and Lower Silesia voivodeships in 2024. In the next chapter, Anita Dmitruczuk examines the problem of environmental management in light of the Oder River poisoning in 2022. The National Disaster Management Plan did not provide procedures in the case of surface water contamination and the environmental disaster triggered a political crisis. This chapter analyzes the political, as well as institutional reasons for the late response to the disaster in an attempt to identify recommendations for the future.

The last two articles concern the issue of knowledge management. Grzegorz Haber writes about data management in local government units in Poland, while Sabina Baraniewicz-Kotasińska focuses on the essential competencies that empower individuals to actively participate in smart city environments and thrive within their dynamic ecosystems, also using the example of crisis communication during the aforementioned flood in 2024.

All chapters address the issue of non-military security challenges for public policies. The authors point out numerous imperfections in the functioning of anti-crisis structures of states during local crises. This issue also influenced the title of this volume. The authors tried to link a broad research perspective with practice and consideration of specific public security challenges.

References

ALDRICH, D. P., *Building Resilience Social Capital in Post-Disaster Recovery*, University of Chicago Press, Chicago 2012. DOI: https://doi.org/10.7208/chicago/9780226012896.001.0001

ALEKSANDROWICZ, T., "Forecasting Threats to State Security in Theory and in Practice. Toolbox for the Analyst", *Internal Security*, Vol. 15, No. 1, 2023, pp. 7–21. DOI: http://dx.doi.org/10.5604/01.3001.0053.9579

ALEXANDER, D. E., "Resilience and Disaster Risk Reduction: An Etymological Journey", *Nat. Hazards Earth Syst. Sci.*, 13, 2013, pp. 2707–2716. https://doi.org/10.5194/nhess-13-2707-2013

AVEN, T., "The risk concept — historical and recent development trends", *Reliability, Engineering and System Safety*, vol. 99 (2012), pp. 33–44. DOI: https://doi.org/10.1016/j.ress.2011.11.006

BECK, U., *Risk Society. Towards a New Modernity*, Sage Publications, London – Newbury Park – New Delhi 1992.

BENNETT, N. & LEMOINE, G. J., *What VUCA Really Means for You*, Harvard Business Review, 2014.

BUZAN, B., WAEVER, O., DE WILDE, J., *Security. A New Framework for Analysis*, Lynne Rienner Publishers, Boulder – London 1998.

COVELLO, V. T., MENKES, J., NEHNEVAJSA, J., "Risk Analysis, Philosophy, and the Social and Behavioral Sciences: Reflections on the Scope of Risk Analysis Research", *Risk Analysis*, Vol. 2, no. 2, 1982, pp. 53–58. DOI: https://doi.org/10.1111/j.1539-6924.1982.tb01366.x

HAY, C., *Political Analysis. A Critical Introduction*, Palgrave Macmillan, London & New York 2002.

INTRIERI, E., DOTTA, J., FONTANELLI, K., BIANCHINI, Ch., BARDI, F., CAMPATELLI, F., CASAGLI, N., "Operational Framework for Flood Risk Communication", *International Journal of Disaster Risk Reduction*. Vol. 46, June 2020. DOI: https://doi.org/10.1016/j.ijdrr.2020.101510

JASANOFF, S., "The political science of risk perception", *Reliability Engineering and System Safety*, vol. 59, 1998, pp. 91–99. DOI: https://doi.org/10.1016/S0951-8320(97)00129-4

KAŁUŻA, T., HÄMMERLING, M., ZAWADZKI, P., CZEKAŁA, W., KASPEREK, R., SOJKA, M., MOKWA, M., PTAK, M., SZKUDLAREK, A.,

CZECHLOWSKI, M., "The hydropower sector in Poland: Historical development and current status", *Renewable and Sustainable Energy Reviews*. Vol. 158, April, 2022. DOI: https://doi.org/10.1016/j.rser.2022.11215

KOBRIN, S. J., "Political Risk: A Review and Reconsideration", *Journal of International Business Studies*, Vol. 10, No. 1 (Spring - Summer, 1979), pp. 67–80. DOI: https://doi.org/10.1057/palgrave.jibs.8490631

LIN, C. A., "Participatory Flood Risk Management and Environmental Sustainability: The Role of Communication Engagement, Severity Beliefs, Mitigation Barriers and Social Efficacy". *Sustainability*, 17, 2844 2025. DOI: https://doi.org/10.3390/su17072844

MARCH, J., OLSEN, J. P., "The New Institutionalism: Organizational Factors in Political Life", *The American Political Science Review*, Vol. 78, No. 3 (Sep., 1984), pp. 734–749. DOI: https://doi.org/10.2307/1961840

MILLAR, C. C., GROWTH, J. M., MAHON, J. F., "Management Innovation in a VUCA World: Challenges and Recommendations", *California Management Review*, 61(1), 2018, pp. 5–14. DOI: https://doi.org/10.1177/0008125618805111

ORTEGA, L. (ed.) *Managing in a VUCA World (Volatility, Uncertainty, Complexity and Ambiguity)*. Murphy & Moore Publishing, 2023.

ROLARSON, E., BRACKEN, L. J., HARDY, R. J., LARGE, A. R. G., "Rethinking Flood Risk Communication", *Natural Hazards*, Vol 92, pp 1665–1686, March 2018. DOI: https://doi.org/10.1007/s11069-018-3273-4

SMITH, C. L., BROOKS, J., *Security Science: The Theory and Practice of Security*, Butterworth-Heinemann, Waldham – Oxford 2013.

VEDBY RASMUSSEN, M., *Risk and Security*, in: *Oxford Research Encyclopedia of International Studies*, Oxford University Press, Oxford – New York 2017. DOI: https://doi.org/10.1093/acrefore/9780190846626.013.290

WIŚNIEWSKI, B., KACZMARCZYK, B. "Opportunity, Challenge, Risk and Threat - Review of Definitions and Relations", *Internal Security*, vol. 9, no. 2, 2017, pp. 23–32. http://dx.doi.org/10.5604/01.3001.0012.1699

WYRĘBEK, H., "National Security Challenges and Threats", *Wiedza Obronna*, 2022, Vol. 279 No. 2, pp. 109–122. DOI: https://doi.org/10.34752/2022-e279

Civil Protection in Central Europe after the Escalation of the Russian-Ukrainian War

Tomasz Pawłuszko[23]

ABSTRACT
The chapter concerns the development of public policies in Central Europe in response to the Russian-Ukrainian war. Due to mass migrations and increased security risks, the countries of the region faced the challenge of modernizing civil protection structures. The author's aim is to answer the questions (1) what changes to civil protection policies were introduced and (2) whether the adaptations led to the emergence of a new model of crisis management. An institutional perspective was used, which was supplemented by an analysis of expert discourse.

Keywords: civil protection, securitization, civil defense, emergency, public policy

Introduction: What is civil protection?

What is civil protection, and why has it become the subject of public policies? What institutions are responsible for crisis management? What non-military challenges does the Russian-Ukrainian war generate for neighboring countries? All these questions require a thoughtful answer. This chapter also aims to answer questions about the processes of adaptation of contemporary states to complex crisis situations of international scope.

The publication is the result of several years of studies focused on the quality of governance in the Central European region. The issue of civil protection in Central Europe has already been the subject of comparative analyses[24]. Poland, the Czech Republic and Hungary were selected for this

[23] University of Opole, Assistant Professor, Department of Governance and Public Policy. https://orcid.org/0000-0002-5572-3199; research fellow in the Łukasiewicz Research Network — ITECH Institute of Innovation and Technology.

[24] R. Szynowski, R. Ščurek, "Crisis Management in Public Administration Units in Poland and Czech Republic. International Comparative Analysis", *Internal Security*, vol. 16, no. 1, 2024, pp. 59–82. DOI: https://doi.org/10.5604/01.3001.0054.7093; Věra - Karin Brázová, "Response of Central European Civil Security Systems to the Economic Crisis", *Central European Journal of Public Policy*, vol. 9, no. 2, 2015, pp. 142–152, DOI: https://doi.org/10.1515/cejpp-2016-0016

analysis because they are countries with a similar development path[25]. During the studies, I used the perspective of new institutionalism, which was useful in order to outline the context of the functioning of large public policy mechanisms[26]. The source base is advanced literature on the subject, which allows for secondary analysis[27]. The basic technique for working with the texts was close reading. This issue I have undertaken has become particularly important due to the need to adapt state structures to emergency situations.

Modern civil protection includes non-military state security systems. The dynamic development of these systems began in the 20th century, when European states began to create institutions that were to protect civilians from the effects of wars, catastrophes and natural disasters[28]. In the second half of the 20th century, civil protection institutions such as civil defense, rescue systems and fire brigades were developed. Their purpose was to warn, alarm and evacuate the population from mass threats[29]. In parallel, formations ensuring public order became separate non-military security systems. Their task is to protect against prohibited actions. These tasks are performed by police formations, intelligence services and various departmental inspections. Modern civil protection in Europe is based on the cooperation of these two

---

25 At the time of preparation of the chapter, the Slovak government did not provide adequate data for a full comparative analysis of the V4 countries; the last data provided to the EU was from 2019. However, the characteristics of the Slovak security system are similar to the contemporary Czech system, as they share a common tradition of statehood from the 20th century, see: S. Kavan, "Provisions of Civil Defence Training in Czechoslovakia – Historical Consequences", *Security Dimensions*, vol. 47, 2024, pp. 44–58. DOI: https://doi.org/10.5604/01.3001.0054.6713

26 J. G. March, J. P. Olsen, "The New Institutionalism: Organizational Factors in Political Life", *The American Political Science Review*, Vol. 78, No. 3 (Sep., 1984), pp. 734–749. DOI: https://doi.org/10.2307/1961840

27 L. Borzillo, D. Deschaux-Dutard, *Secondary Analysis of Qualitative Data in Defense Studies: Methodological Opportunities and Challenges*, in: *Research Methods in Defense Studies. A Multidisciplinary Overview*, Edited by Delphine Deschaux-Dutard, Routledge, London & New York 2021, pp. 60–75. DOI: https://doi.org/10.4324/9780429198236

28 M. Kopczewski, P. Szmitkowski, "Civil Defense In Poland – Transformation Process After 1989. Current State And Modernization Proposals", *De Securitate et Defensione*, No. 1 (6) 2020, pp. 75–87. DOI: https://doi.org/10.34739/dsd.2020.01.04

29 A. Skrabacz, A. Pajka, B. Więckowski, "Crisis Management as a Research Province of Security Science", *Roczniki Nauk Społecznych*, vol. 16, no. 1, 2024, pp. 7–25, DOI: https://doi.org/10.18290/rns2024.0010

groups of institutions. Their basic function is to manage crises in peacetime. In times of crisis and war, however, they gain additional tasks.

The origins of civil protection institutions

The basic historical context for the development of civil protection institutions is the growing risk of victims of international conflicts and crises. During World War I, almost 10 million people died, and the ratio of soldiers killed to civilians was approximately 10 to 1. During World War II, 47 million of the 72 million killed were civilians. Both world wars were fought largely on the territory of Central European countries. Another context is the development of technology that enables the production of lethal weapons with a large range of destruction, which increases the risk for civilians who do not take direct part in armed combat. It is currently estimated that for every soldier killed, there are as many as ten civilians killed[30]. Modern warfare is no longer just a problem for fighting armies. The increasing power and range of modern weapons allows for hitting numerous targets and destroying the economies of entire countries. Weapons of mass destruction have also appeared. States counteract the risk of civilian casualties in two ways. The first is international regulations, and the second is the creation of civil defense systems.

In 1949, four so-called Geneva Conventions were adopted: 1) For the Amelioration of the Condition of the Wounded and Sick in Armed Forces in the Field, 2) For the Amelioration of the Condition of the Wounded, Sick and Shipwrecked at Sea, 3) On the Treatment of Prisoners of War, and 4) On the Protection of Civilians in Time of War. These provisions were expanded in 1977 by two additional protocols. In their light, civil defense aims to protect the civilian population from dangers resulting from military operations or natural disasters and to overcome their immediate consequences.

Article 61 presents a list of tasks for states that want to create effective protection for the population in times of peace, crisis and war. The box

[30] R. Kalinowski, *Obrona Cywilna w Polsce*, Uniwersytet w Siedlcach, Siedlce 2017, pp. 11–41.

below indicates that to fulfill these tasks, states must design a total of several advanced mechanisms for cooperation between different rescue services.

Table 1: Civil defense tasks

1. Warning service
2. Evacuation
3. Preparing and organizing shelters
4. Handling of shading agents
5. Rescue
6. Medical services, first aid and religious care
7. Fighting fires
8. Detection and marking of dangerous zones
10. Disinfection and similar protective measures
11. Providing emergency rooms and supplies
12. Emergency assistance to restore order
13. Emergency restoration of public utility services
14. Improper burial of the dead
15. Help in saving goods necessary for survival
16. Additional types of activities, including planning and organizational work

Source: Chapter VI, Article 61 of the First Protocol additional to the Geneva Conventions of 12 August 1949, and relating to the Protection of Victims of International Armed Conflicts, Geneva, 8 June 1977.

In post-war Europe, two models of civil protection could be distinguished. In Western Europe, a civilian system of protection against natural disasters and catastrophes was created. Meanwhile, in the communist countries of Eastern Europe, a militarized civil defense system was organized to protect the population in the event of a nuclear war.

After the collapse of the Eastern Bloc, Eastern European countries began to adapt their systems to the Western model. It was assumed that another war in Europe was unlikely. Rescue systems became decentralized, and former Warsaw Pact member states joined the Geneva Conventions regime and demilitarized their rescue structures. The main changes in the population protection systems of countries such as Poland, Hungary, and the Czech Republic were: (1) a departure from military-type planning and defense against weapons of mass destruction in favor of a universal approach; (2) opening up to civil administration and society; and (3) replacing military with civilian personnel.

The security culture also changed. The emergence of civilian mechanisms introduced other management patterns into public structures. Inspired by the ideas of new public management, managerial elements began to be introduced into public administration instead of military ones[31]. Even the name "civil defense" itself began to be replaced by "crisis management". The former civil defense structures were gradually replaced by other peacetime rescue systems. The main rescue mechanism was precisely crisis management, which integrated public administration systems with public services provided by rescue services. Civil defense, on the other hand, was to become a mechanism for cooperation between rescue services and civil public administration in the event of crises, natural disasters and wars. At the turn of the millennium, there was therefore demilitarization, defragmentation and deregulation of population protection systems. Civil defense tasks were taken over by small professional structures.

Currently, there are at least three general models of organizing the civil protection systems in Europe[32]. The first model comes from the Cold War and is etatist. This model is based on the militarization of civil defense structures. This is a costly model and often requires the establishment of a separate ministry and separate protective formations. Structures similar to this model operate today in Spain, France, and Russia. The second model is based on expanding the financing and competences of rescue services, which have material reserves in case of crises. This situation occurs in Germany, Hungary, and Poland. The third model is the Scandinavian model, which is

---

31 G. Kunikowski, K. Rostek, "Good practices in civil planning and crisis management in the world and their implementation in Poland", *Jagiellonian Journal of Management*, vol. 3 (2017), no. 3, pp. 135–150. DOI: https://doi.org/10.4467/2450114XJJM.17.009.9560; G. Pietrek, "The crisis management system and the civil protection system. Similarities, differences, possibilities of standardization", *Security and Defense Quarterly*, vol. 16, no. 3/2017, pp. 75–88. DOI: https://doi.org/10.35467/sdq/103185

32 See: *The national disaster management system*, European Commission. https://civil-protection-humanitarian-aid.ec.europa.eu/what/civil-protection/national-disaster-management-system_en; other models are mentioned in: *The Structure, Role and Mandate of Civil Protection in Disaster Risk Reduction for South Eastern Europe South Eastern Europe Disaster Risk Mitigation and Adaptation Program*, United Nations Office for the Coordination of Humanitarian Affairs (OCHA), Emergency Preparedness Section Palais des Nations, Geneva 2009. https://www.undrr.org/publication/structure-role-and-mandate-civil-protection-disaster-risk-reduction-south-eastern

based on mass training of citizens to support a small number of professional protective formations. This concept is popular in countries with a small population.

The end of the Cold War did not mean that mass threats to civilians disappeared. Today, there are at least two types of problems with civil protection systems. These are external and internal problems. The first result from threats, and the second result from the shape of security institutions. In the first decade of the 21st century, EU authorities were mainly afraid of fires and floods. In the second decade of the 21st century, the catalogue of threats has expanded significantly. In addition to natural disasters and catastrophes, problems related to mass movements of people (uncontrolled migration, refugees, mass hospitalization, conflicts) appeared[33]. These problems required a response from ministries responsible for internal security. The war in Ukraine has become a cumulation of existing challenges on an unprecedented scale.

The issue of civil protection has also become an important element of cooperation between states in the European Union. In October 2001, the European Commission established the EU Civil Protection Mechanism. A few years later, the Lisbon Treaty raised civil protection to the level of EU fundamental rights. The legal basis for EU cooperation in the prevention of natural disasters is Article 196 of the Lisbon Treaty. However, civil protection remains the responsibility of the Member States, while the EU plays a supporting and coordinating role. In 2013–2014, the EU Civil Protection Mechanism was reformed, and, among other things, the Emergency Response Coordination Centre (ERCC) was established[34]. In Europe, civil protection focuses on supporting states in such matters as: supplies (medicines, shelter elements, water purification), organisation of rescue support, analytical

---

[33] L. Teknős, "Analysis and Assessment of the Growing Tendencies of Natural Disasters and Events in Hungary from the Perspective of Disaster Management", *Security Dimensions*, vol. 43, no. 43, 2022, pp. 53–75. DOI: https://doi.org/10.5604/01.3001.0054.1483

[34] *Civil Protection*, European Civil Protection and Humanitarian Aid Operations, European Commission. https://civil-protection-humanitarian-aid.ec.europa.eu/what/civil-protection_en

support and repatriation of EU citizens[35]. One of the main principles on which this mechanism is based is solidarity[36].

According to the latest EU statistics, from 1980 to 2022, natural hazards affected over 50 million people and cost Member States €650 billion in total (of which €59 billion in 2021 and €52 billion in 2022)[37]. In recent years, the COVID-19 pandemic and the war in Ukraine have led to increased cooperation between Member States and strengthened the position of institutions responsible for protecting civilians[38]. By the end of 2024, the EU Civil Protection Mechanism had been activated over 770 times. According to the European Commission, disaster risk management considerations have been incorporated into key EU policy areas, including health, environment, climate change adaptation, development, cohesion, agriculture, transport, energy, research, and innovation. Within the mechanism, European countries supported Ukraine and made their resources available to partners, as none of them had created a fully self-sufficient civil protection system.

Problems of civil protection in Central Europe

Poland, the Czech Republic and Hungary inherited their civil protection systems from the communist era. Concerns about the participation of the Eastern Bloc countries in a nuclear war led to the development of civil defence

---

35 Ch. Parker, T. Persson, S. Widmalm, "The Effectiveness of National and EU-level Civil Protection Systems: Evidence from 17 Member States", *Journal of European Public Policy*, vol. 26, issue 9, 2019, pp. 1312–1334. https://doi.org/10.1080/13501763.2018.1523219

36 A. Boin, M. Rhinard, "Crisis management performance and the European Union: the case of COVID-19", *Journal of European Public Policy*, 2023, Vol. 30, No. 4, pp. 655–675; DOI: https://doi.org/10.1080/13501763.2022.2141304; M. Malešič, "The Union Civil Protection Mechanism in the Prism of Solidarity Theory", *Journal of Comparative Politics*, vol. 18, no. 1, 2025, pp. 34–50.

37 European Disaster and Risk Management, European Commission. https://civil-protection-humanitarian-aid.ec.europa.eu/what/civil-protection/european-disaster-risk-management_en

38 A. Turska-Kawa, P. Csanyi, R. Kucharčík, "From the "Rally 'Round The Flag" Effect to a Social Crisis of Confidence. Poland and Slovakia in the First Year of the Covid-19 Pandemic", *Journal of Comparative Politics*, vol. 15, no. 1, 2022, pp. 20–38; V. Prebilič, "Crisis Management in Municipality: The Role Of Civil Protection During Covid-19 Crisis", *Journal of Comparative Politics*, vol. 15, no. 1, 2022, pp. 56–72.

institutions[39]. Civil defence was militarised, and its task was to ensure the safety of civilians during heightened states of defence readiness. In peacetime, civil defence dealt with rescue and planning activities. In communist countries, civil defence did not include, for example, terrorism, combating crime or epidemics, because it was believed that these threats remained the same in both war and peace. As a result, the civil defence system did not gain the same importance as the army and police. It was more of a militarised system of cooperation between various institutions in states of higher defence readiness, rather than a separate organisation[40]. After the end of the Cold War, reforms of the civil defence system began towards its demilitarisation. The subject of civil protection was transferred from the ministries of defence to the ministries of internal affairs. The main stages of changes in the Central European civil protection systems are outlined below.

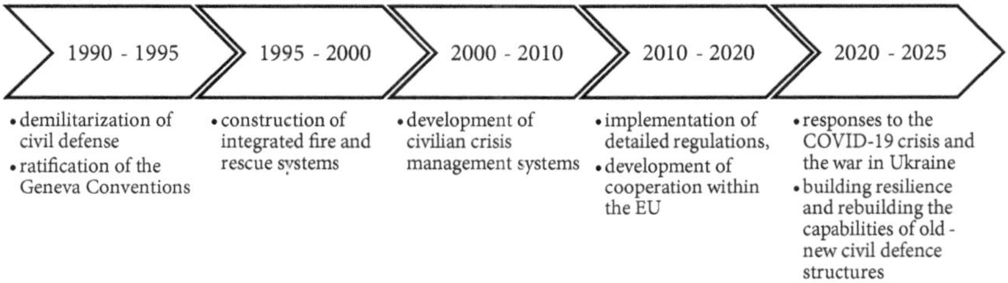

Graph 1: Stages of development of civil protection systems in Central Europe after 1989.
Source: own study.

The countries of Central Europe modernized their internal security institutions at a similar pace and in a similar manner. The first comprehensive regulations covered rescue structures. The next step was the statutory regulation of crisis management systems, which took place at the turn of the 20th and 21st centuries. The countries began to analyze the risk of threats to a greater extent and adapt local structures to the new systems. In subsequent

[39] *Civil protection in Hungary*, June 2009. https://www.iaem.org/portals/25/documents/HungaryEM.pdf
[40] G. Sobolewski, "Systemic Approach to Civil Protection in Poland", *Safety and Fire Technology*, vol. 54 (2), 2019, pp. 116–131. DOI: https://www.doi.org/10.12845/sft.54.2.2019.9

years, the countries of the region adapted their institutions to NATO and EU requirements, which led, among other things, to the establishment of professional armies, the abolition of conscription and the adoption of laws on combating terrorism. The issue of civil protection in peacetime became the task of professional rescue services, which were to support local authorities. In accordance with the principle of subsidiarity, most new crisis management systems assumed that central and regional authorities would provide additional material support for regions temporarily affected by floods, fires, droughts, or storms. The states' authorities also recognized that war in the region was unlikely, so training the population in civil defense practices was no longer a priority. The next stage was to regulate the problem of cybersecurity and strengthen cooperation between states in the field of disaster prevention (fires, floods).

After 2015, hybrid warfare and international migration became important topics in the European debate. After 2020, non-military threats intensified. Countries in the region fought the effects of the pandemic and made efforts to accommodate the multi-million refugees from war-torn Ukraine. Below, I discuss the main problems of public policies in the Czech Republic, Poland, and Hungary.

The Czech Republic

In the Czech Republic, an act regulating the basic elements of the civil protection system was adopted in 2000. On the basis of the Crisis Act, the Czech Republic could declare 4 crisis states: a state of danger, a state of emergency, a state of peril, and a state of war. The states are declared by the regional governor (a state of danger), government (a state of emergency), parliament on proposal of the government (a state of peril), or parliament (state of war). To strengthen the response to major emergencies resulting from the most significant risks, the Czech Republic also develops 16 documents in the form of a checklist, which describes such an emergency and appropriate measures to ensure an effective response[41]. All the documents are available on the website of the Ministry of Interior - Directorate General of the Fire

---

[41] Czech Republic, European Civil Protection and Humanitarian Aid Operations. https://civil-protection-humanitarian-aid.ec.europa.eu/what/civil-protection/national-disaster-management-system/czech-republic_en

Rescue Service of Czechia (MoI – DG FRS CR). The act obliges rescue units to operate both in peacetime and in wartime (Article 39), unless other regulations provide otherwise[42].

The Czech civil protection system is dominated by fire brigades, whose competences were expanded after 2015. The system remains demilitarized[43]. Each fire station and each regional FRS have their own exercise plans, which are coordinated at the national level to ensure that other services (regional Emergency Medical Services, EMS), the police, army and other bodies of the Integrated Rescue System of the Czech Republic (IRS CR) are incorporated into these plans.

Firefighter units are part of the Integrated Rescue System of the Czech Republic, which is designed to coordinate rescue during emergencies[44]. This system has been developed in the Czech Republic since 2001. Today it includes fire protection units, EMS providers and the police. The Czech Republic is divided into 14 separate territorial areas, and each of them is operated by the regional headquarters of the FRS, which administers its regional operational center. These emergency centers can receive emergency calls from the national emergency number.

In 2023, the Czech Republic adopted a new National Security Strategy, which defines civil protection systems as the basis for the resilience of society (point 7). These systems are one of the elements of the internal security of the Czech Republic, and their maintenance remains a vital national interest (point 17). The Czech government declared the reinforcement of rescue formation equipment (point 54) and cooperation with other countries within the framework of EU mechanisms (point 58). Key provisions concern the preparation of the system in the event of war and nuclear attack. In accordance with NATO concepts, the Czech Republic declared seven baseline requirements for national resilience: (1) assured continuity of government,

---

42 Crisis Management Act N. 240/2000 Coll. https://ec.europa.eu/echo/files/civil_protection/national_disaster_management_system/czech_republic/239_2000_irs_cz_act.pdf

43 Act N. 320/2015 Coll. of 11 November 2015 on the Fire Rescue Service of the Czech Republic and on amendment of certain acts (Act on the Fire Rescue Service). https://ec.europa.eu/echo/files/civil_protection/national_disaster_management_system/czech_republic/320_2015_frs_cz_act.pdf

44 *Czechia – Civil Protection*, European Committee of the Regions. https://portal.cor.europa.eu/divisionpowers/Pages/Czechia-Civil-Protection.aspx

(2) resilient energy supplies, (3) the ability to deal effectively with uncontrolled movement of people, (4) resilient water and food resources, (5) the ability to deal with mass casualties, (6) resilient civil communications systems, and (7) resilient transport systems. The final provisions on civil protection are contained in the Strategy in a separate chapter as "civil protection and crisis management" (points 121–125).

The key change in the perception of civil protection problems was the devastating Russian invasion of Ukraine. The Czech strategy indicates that Russia's actions undermine the security of the Czech Republic and NATO. The National Security Council, chaired by the Prime Minister, is responsible for the entire Czech security system[45]. The Rules of Procedure of the National Security Council are publicly available. The hierarchical decision-making system controls approximately 7,000 local crisis management units[46].

Poland

Poland is a relatively large country, which is why peacetime and wartime security systems have long been differentiated. The peacetime crisis management system was standardized in 2007, while the regulations on population protection in wartime did not come into force until 2025. For years, reforms of the old civil defense system have failed[47].

After 1989, Polish governments first began to reform the peacetime protection systems. The establishment of the National Rescue and Firefighting System (1995) and the adoption of the Crisis Management Act (2007) were key. At the same time, the head of the National Civil Defense (Obrona Cywilna Kraju, OCK) did not receive a separate office and did not become the superior of the heads of regional structures (they were voivodes). In 2007,

---

45 National Security Council, Government of the Czech Republic. https://vlada.gov.cz/en/ppov/brs/office-of-the-government-of-the-czech-republic-23851/

46 T. Ivanuša, I. Podbregar, E. Bakoš, F. Božek, *Integrated Rescue System in the Czech Republic and in the Republic of Slovenia: Similarities / Differences – Advantages / Disadvantages*, Conference Paper: 5th International Conference "Crisis management days", Velika Gorica, Croatia, May 2012. https://www.researchgate.net/publication/281859686_Integrated_Rescue_System_in_the_Czech_Republic_and_in_the_Republic_of_Slovenia_Similarities_Differences_-_Advantages_Disadvantages

47 R. Ostrowska, "Civil defense in Poland from a historical perspective", *Scientific Journal of the Military University of Land Forces*, 2021, Volume 53, Number 3 (201), pp. 496–506. DOI: https://doi.org/ 10.5604/01.3001.0015.3402

a separate crisis management system was organized, which was based on the Government Centre for Security (RCB)[48]. As in the Czech Republic, a crisis management system was organized in each voivodeship, district and commune under the management of local authorities.

Civil defense remained on the margin of interest of Polish governments until the outbreak of the Russian-Ukrainian conflict in the period 2014–2015[49]. However, despite a decade (!) of war, Poland failed to pass regulations during this time, also despite the occurrence of other crises threatening millions of Polish residents (pandemic, floods, mass migrations, escalation of the war and the risk of its spillover into the region). Subsequent bills (2014, 2016, 2019, 2022) were not passed for reasons such as lack of agreement in the government, lack of financial resources, or the end of the parliament's term. During this time, the remnants of the OCK were systematically degraded, as reported by the Supreme Audit Office (NIK) in subsequent audits[50]. The above omissions of Polish governments remain inconsistent with doctrinal documents in the field of Poland's national security. The Strategy for the Development of the Security System of the Republic of Poland, the White Paper on National Security and both National Security Strategies from 2014 and 2020 recommended repairing the civil protection system. The recommendations were not implemented.

In 2020–2022, Poland was hit by numerous crises. In 2021, a crisis broke out on the Polish-Belarusian border. On February 24, 2022, Russia carried out a full-scale invasion of Ukraine. The Polish government was unprepared for the wave of refugees, so the main burden of aid fell on local governments and private citizens. In the spring of 2022, Poland abolished the Civil Defense, but failed to adopt new regulations. In 2022, the Government Legislation

---

48 *Government Centre for Security*. https://www.gov.pl/web/rcb

49 Does Poland need civil defense? February 8, 2013. https://www.nik.gov.pl/en/news/does-poland-need-civil-defence-part-1.html

50 In March 2012, NIK announced *the Information on the results of the audit entitled Preparation of civil defense structures to carry out tasks in times of war and peace*. https://www.nik.gov.pl/en/news/nik-on-civil-defence.html In June 2013, NIK announced *the Information on the results of the audit entitled Preparation of the system for protecting the population against natural disasters and crisis situations*. https://www.nik.gov.pl/en/news/nik-on-crisis-management-2013.html At the turn of 2018 and 2019, NIK announced *the Information on the results of the audit entitled Protection of the population within the framework of crisis management and civil defense*. See: Supreme Audit Office. https://www.nik.gov.pl/en/

Center published drafts of a new *Act on the Protection of the Population and on the State of Natural Disaster*, the adoption of which would restore the existence of civil defense. The draft announced extra-constitutional states of emergency, the strengthening of the Government Crisis Management Team, the establishment of the Civil Protection Fund outside parliamentary control, the liquidation of the Government Centre for Security, and the establishment of the State Duty Service. The bill was submitted for review, but it was not passed until the end of the parliament's term in 2023. After the start of the new parliamentary term, work on the (new!) bill began again.

At the end of 2024, civil defense was resurrected in Poland. The new Act on Civil Protection and Civil Defense (*Ustawa o Ochronie Ludności i Obronie Cywilnej*) came into force in January 2025[51]. The new system is based on the previous rescue formations, but many new institutions have been introduced[52]. The correct decision-making and planning system has been restored, the role of the Government Security Centre has been strengthened, the universal training system has been restored, and sustainable financing has been ensured (for this purpose, the government has been announcing regular The Civil Protection and Civil Defense Program). The Act defines the authorities, entities and resources of the new system. The civil protection system will have a new inventory of resources and will implement a new state communication system. A new system of shelters for the civilian population will be built from scratch because the devastated shelter system from the Cold War era does not meet modern requirements. In the event of war, the Civil Defense Corps (Korpus Obrony Cywilnej, KOC) will be recreated, which will be based on former police, guard and military officers. The Act will be subject to revision every two years. There is an ongoing debate in Poland on

---

51 *Poland introduces "landmark" new civil defense law*, Notes from Poland, December 19, 2024. https://notesfrompoland.com/2024/12/19/poland-introduces-landmark-new-civil-defence-law/; original legal act was published in https://orka.sejm.gov.pl/proc10.nsf/ustawy/664_u.htm

52 This part of the text is based on my conference presentation, Tomasz Pawłuszko, *Perspectives of the development of population protection systems. Comments on new regulations*. The presentation was recorded at the 5th National Scientific Conference "Internal security and its contexts", 23/01/2025, at the Center for Research Methodology in Security Sciences at the WSB University in Poland.

the efficiency of the system and the missing detailed regulations (the new Act requires the adoption of over 20 additional regulations).

Hungary

In Hungary, the Civil Defense Act was adopted in 1996. Then, in 1999, the National Directorate General for Disaster Management (BM OKF, Belügyminisztérium Országos Katasztrófavédelmi Főigazgatóság) was established[53]. The structure was established in the Ministry of the Interior. It currently operates on the basis of the reformed act of 2011[54]. This institution is based on the demilitarized competences of the fire service[55]. In the operational structure, the key decision-making bodies are the Inspectorate General of Firefighting and the Inspectorate General of Civil Protection[56]. The central office is responsible for local fire service structures, supported by local government and non-governmental organizations[57]. The Directorate General is responsible for fire protection and civil protection and can use a large pool of assets for this purpose (which its Polish counterpart does not have). The Directorate is responsible for civil crisis planning and defense management. It regulates and manages the fire brigade system, technical rescue, material reserves and public information (prevention and training). It also deals with water protection and the safety of civil nuclear energy[58].

---

53 *Belügyminisztérium Országos Katasztrófavédelmi Főigazgatóság*, 11/08/2024. https://www.katasztrofavedelem.hu/2/bemutatkozas

54 *2011. évi CXXVIII. törvény - a katasztrófavédelemről és a hozzá kapcsolódó egyes törvények módosításáról*. https://civil-protection-humanitarian-aid.ec.europa.eu/system/files/2022-06/act_on_disaster_management_CXXVIII_2011_en.pdf

55 J. Ambrusz, *The System of Disaster Preparedness in Hungary*, in: *Educating for Democratic Governance and Global Citizenship*, World Council for Curriculum and Instruction, San Diego 2016, pp. 231–235; L. Kozári, *System of Hungarian System Management*, Defense Technical Information Center Compilation Part Notice, ADP013436 (Unclassified). https://apps.dtic.mil/sti/tr/pdf/ADP013436.pdf

56 M. Novaky, L. Katai-Urban, "Development of Civil Protection in Hungary", *Зарубежный опыт: гражданская защита*, pp. 89–95. DOI: https://doi.org/10.25257/FE.2018.1.89-95 https://cyberleninka.ru/article/n/development-of-civil-protection-in-hungary

57 This part of the chapter is based on my previous analysis: T. Pawłuszko, *Civil Protection in Poland and Hungary. Searching for good practices*, Sobieski Institute, 12 August 2024. https://sobieski.org.pl/en/civil-protection-in-poland-and-hungary-searching-for-good-practices/

58 *Hatósági tevékenység ismertetése*, 10/08/2024. https://www.katasztrofavedelem.hu/78/hatosagi-tevekenyseg-ismertetese

It supervises the preparation of local and plant plans. It also cooperates with law enforcement agencies[59].

In April 2020, the Hungarian government adopted a new National Security Strategy[60], and in June 2021, Hungary's National Military Strategy was passed. This was followed by new defense regulations, such as Act XCIII on the Coordination of Defense and Security Activities[61]. This led to a deeper connection between the defense system and civil protection by strengthening the security of critical infrastructure facilities.

Currently, the Hungarian General Directorate has at its disposal regional training bases, the Disaster Management Education Centre, the Disaster Management Institute of the State Higher School of Public Services, the Disaster Management Museum and the Disaster Management Research Institute. In addition, it publishes a monthly magazine and teaching materials, organizes education and runs a sports association. Most similar structures in Poland have practically not existed for years or have operated independently of the Government Centre for Security. Poland is a larger country, and therefore its system is decentralized and based on regional crisis management centres. In a crisis, local authorities are to manage the network of professional organizations and take care of the evacuation and alarming of the population. The fire brigade has a subordinate role in the Polish system. However, the lessons from the Ukrainian war indicate that such a system may be ineffective in the event of an armed conflict. The fire brigade does not have the competence to build shelters, create evacuation points, warn, alarm or transport goods. In the event of a conflict, firefighters will perform their basic firefighting tasks.

The Hungarian civil protection system is clearer and has a clear legal basis, competence structure and institutional background. The scale of the challenges remains significant, however, because the Hungarian rescue system

---

59 V. Petkov, T. Tagarev, "Hungary: Capabilities, Organizations, Policies, and Legislation in crisis management and disaster response", *Connections. The Quarterly Journal*, ITSec4 Reports 127, Sofia, March 2015. https://connections-qj.org/article/hungary-capabilities-organizations-policies-and-legislation-crisis-management-and-disaster

60 Government Resolution 1163/2020 (21st April) on Hungary's National Security Strategy. https://honvedelem.hu/hirek/government-resolution-1163-2020-21st-april.html

61 M. Novaky, "Hungary's Disaster Management Tasks in the Light of the Challenges of Defense and Security in the 21st Century", *Security Dimensions*, no. 42, 2022, pp. 36–47. DOI: https://doi.org/ 10.5604/01.3001.0016.0734

also deals with nuclear power, water supply, safety engineering, industrial supervision, training and certification. The system seems well prepared to respond to technical threats and in the event of natural disasters (floods, fires, failures).

The main problem of Hungary, as well as Poland, is the insufficient preparation to respond to mass movements of people (mass evacuation or uncontrolled migration). Both Poland and Hungary have had to use the military in recent years to deal with migration and health crises. The military is an external security institution, it is not subordinate to the Ministry of Interior, and it does not have sufficient police or order powers. Therefore, there is still room for improvement in the development of civil protection personnel and increasing the involvement of NGOs and citizens.

The war in Ukraine and the problems of civil protection systems in Central Europe

In February 2022, Russia's full-scale invasion of Ukraine triggered the fastest-growing displacement crisis in the world. Millions of people were forced to leave Ukraine, while millions more were displaced within the country. The majority of those fleeing Ukraine were women and children. In 2025, about 3.5 million people are believed to be internally displaced. Meanwhile, many others are still stranded in affected areas, either unwilling or unable to leave due to military action. An estimated 12.7 million people needed humanitarian assistance in 2025[62].

The Russian invasion of Ukraine has triggered a need for reforms in European civil protection systems[63]. This need is particularly strong in the region of Central and Eastern Europe, which is located in the territory of the former Soviet Union. The Russian military has often deliberately bombed critical infrastructure facilities, power plants, schools, hospitals,

---

62 Ukraine report, European Commission. https://civil-protection-humanitarian-aid.ec.europa.eu/where/europe/ukraine_en

63 J. Kompan, M. Hrnčiar, "The Security Sector Reform of the Fragile State as a Tool for Conflict Prevention", *Politické Vedy*, Vol. 24, No. 2, 2021 pp. 87–107. DOI: https://doi.org/10.24040/politickevedy.2021.24.2.87-107 S. Kowalkowski, M. Wrzosek, D. Kaźmierczak, "Challenges to Civil Protection in Times of Future Wars", *Wiedza Obronna*, vol. 284, no. 3, 2023. DOI: https://doi.org/10.34752/2023-a284

and housing estates, which has been widely documented by the news media and has become a warning to civil protection managers throughout Europe. Practically the entire catalog of former civil defense tasks, included in the Additional Protocol to the Geneva Conventions, has once again become a problem of public policies. Civil protection is no longer seen through the prism of solving minor local crises but requires the commitment of resources on a national policy scale.

The sections above briefly discuss the origins and shape of the protection systems in the Czech Republic, Poland, and Hungary. In this part of the chapter, I will try to identify the main institutional challenges for these systems from the perspective of (1) the problems to date and (2) the threats observed in Ukraine. The challenges from the first perspective have been reconstructed based on an in-depth analysis of the literature and the author's practical experience. The results are presented in Box 2.

Table 2: Civil defence tasks and challenges for population protection in Central Europe

Catalogue of civil defense tasks	Current challenges for civil protection in Central Europe
Warning service	Countries in the region have 24-hour warning institutions
Evacuation	Countries in the region theoretically have evacuation plans, but not all of them. There is a lack of shelters and designated evacuation sites
Preparing shelters	The shelters in the countries of the region can only accommodate a dozen or so percent of the population.
Handling of shading agents	Due to the development of technology, the task has lost its importance
Rescue	All countries in the region have numerous rescue units, both professional and voluntary. However, there are still vacancies.
Medical services	The countries of the region have medical infrastructure, but there is a lack of doctors, nurses and rescue vehicles.
Fire-fighting	Rescue formations have operational reserves that can be directed to firefighting tasks.

(Continued)

Table 2: *(Continued)*

Catalogue of civil defense tasks	Current challenges for civil protection in Central Europe
Detection and marking of dangerous zones	Engineering tasks can be performed by rescue and military (sapper) services with the support of the police (staff shortages)
Disinfection	Military and rescue units have chemical and engineering units, but only in small numbers.
Providing emergency rooms and supplies	This task is the responsibility of local authorities, which often do not have the strength and financial resources to obtain supplies and need support.
Emergency assistance to restore order	This task is carried out by local authorities with the support of the police, but in the absence of supplies, shelters and hiding places, it may be difficult to organize
Emergency restoration of public utility services	In the event of an armed conflict, most uniformed services will be unavailable to local authorities because they will be performing other statutory tasks.
Help in saving goods necessary for survival	The civilian population is poorly informed about the principles of protection, alerting and evacuation, which may make it difficult to save property
Additional activities, including planning and organizing	Crisis management plans are often incomplete or not based on reality.

Source: Own study based on Chapter VI, Article 61 of the I Protocol Additional to the Geneva Conventions of 12 August 1949, and Relating to the Protection of Victims of International Armed Conflicts, Geneva, 8 June 1977.

The above list does not disregard the fact that the countries of Central Europe have created effective rescue and firefighting systems, and also have well-maintained infrastructure, equipment and experience in counteracting the effects of natural disasters. However, we have already noticed that for local structures to operate effectively, the right context is needed, which is a strong legal and political framework of the state. The previous analysis indicated the reactivity of decision-making factors, which probably influenced the slow transformation of civil protection systems. These processes have been going on for several decades and are still not completed, and in the case of Poland, the institutional transformation was launched only after 2025.

At this point, we can hypothesize that the observed deficits and institutional problems result from weaknesses in the design of political institutions. Decision-makers have problems with knowledge management in such a difficult area of public policy as security. The low political attractiveness of this field of knowledge means that the possibilities for institutional change have been limited. Politicians do not use or do not implement the analytical tools they have, such as foresight. Recent years have also shown a relatively small number of scientific publications and think tank reports on the subject of civil protection. Until the outbreak of the Russian-Ukrainian war, this topic did not interest either political scientists or soldiers. As a result, the needs of states were not properly recognized, legal acts were not prepared, and institutions are still not ready to act. The effects of these deficits are destructive for the state system, for which ensuring the safety of citizens is a fundamental political task. The consequences are, for example, (1) lack of a stable security management system, (2) decision-making chaos in the planning process, (3) many years of stagnation in the modernization of the armed forces, (4) staffing problems of many security institutions, or (5) the breakdown of some civil protection systems, including civil defense. It is on these that resilience is usually based[64].

The rapid increase in defense spending in Central European countries results from the priority given to the armed forces and defense infrastructure[65]. It should be added, however, that equally important non-military systems have not had similar support from decision-makers for years. The crisis management systems that have been in place for years are chronically underfunded and base their long-term effectiveness de facto on the expectation of temporary support from central authorities. However, in the event of a nationwide crisis, support may not be available to all institutions. An efficient non-military system would not only allow the population to be saved from poisoning, starvation and bombing, but would also enable long-term support for both its own and allied forces. Furthermore, while the military

---

64 *Resilience in NATO*, December 15, 2023. https://www.act.nato.int/article/resilience-in-nato/

65 J. Piotrowska-Michalak, "Defence tasks carried out by local governments in Poland", *De Securitate et Defensione*, 2 (6) 2020, pp. 185–204. DOI: https://doi.org/10.34739/dsd.2020.02.13; P. Krzykowski, "Defense Infrastructure - an Attempt at Identification", *Security and Defense Quarterly*, vol. 22, 2018, pp. 71–98. DOI: https://doi.org/10.5604/01.3001.0012.7589

subsystem of state security has political support and comprehensive legal regulations, the non-military subsystem has remained underfunded and without support for decades[66]. This means that in situations of threats and higher states of defense readiness, local authorities may be deprived of the means to counteract major crises.

Over the years, numerous obstacles have been growing in the development of the background for civil protection systems. In the literature on the subject, experts often point to the dispersion of law, unpredictable threats, high costs, lack of financial resources and low staffing levels of protection formations. Problems also include inconsistency of procedures, lack of investment, poor information flow and dispersion of tasks.

In addition to the "hard" elements of public policy, "soft" elements, such as education and the culture of population safety, should be taken into account[67]. An important and often ignored context for the operation of civil protection institutions is the situational awareness of citizens. Due to many years of peace, the state's decision-making system during a crisis remains unknown to citizens. Universal training systems also require reconstruction[68]. Existing rescue systems are modern, but they struggle with staffing problems (age, staff salaries) and an excess of tasks.

On the one hand, crisis situations that Ukraine is struggling with cannot be solved with ad hoc solutions. On the other hand, it is worth noting that contemporary non-military threats can be just as devastating as warfare. The example of floods or epidemics, generating billions of USD in losses, encourages us to take non-military threats seriously. In the face of Russia's aggressive policy, the protection system must be based on resources, mechanisms and decision-making procedures analogous to the military system. The system must also be widely known among citizens who, in the absence of limited

---

66 E. Jakubiak, "Coordination and Operation National Emergency and Fire System in Poland", *National Security Studies*, vol. 18, 2020, pp. 35–43. DOI: https://doi.org/10.37055/sbn/145295

67 A. W. Filipek, "Security Culture as a Challenge for Uniformed Services and Other Citizens", *Internal Security*, Vol. 12, No. 2, 2020, pp. 7–19. DOI: https://doi.org/10.5604/01.3001.0014.6655

68 I wrote more about this in: T. Pawłuszko, "Crisis of Civil Defense in Poland. Institutional Perspective", *National Security Studies*, vol. 30, 4/2023, pp. 41–62. DOI: https://doi.org/10.37055/sbn/175516

rescue, police and military formations, might have to perform numerous protective tasks for which they must be trained and equipped.

Summary and recommendations

The author's aim was to answer the question (1) what changes of civil protection policies were introduced and (2) whether the adaptations led to the emergence of a new model of crisis management. The answer to the first question concerns the main thrust of my argument. Central European countries gradually created modern rescue systems of a specialist nature. However, the development of complex threats such as mass migration, war and pandemic has revealed the limitations of this model. Professional but decentralized civil protection systems struggle with small human and material resources. Previous crisis management systems seemed effective in controlling the effects of local non-military risks. However, the increase in the scale of risk and the severity of threats requires the involvement of central authorities and the expansion of population protection systems by further levels of activity. This requires a strategy of action and additional resources. This is a major challenge for public policies in Central Europe.

The answer to the second question is an extension of the above issue. It seems that the countries of Central Europe have not yet developed a new model of public policy in the field of civil protection. At the same time, there is a noticeable reference to practices from the time of etatism in the 20th century. Centralization is growing (nationwide strategies, training systems, digital applications, etc.). In response to new crises, civil protection systems have received many more resources than in the past, and they are also using new technologies that will allow a smaller number of formations to be more effective than the Cold War civil defense systems. However, the system's efficiency and mobilization capacity remain key problems.

This study was an attempt to answer questions about the conditions of development of civil protection systems in Central Europe during the Russian-Ukrainian war. After conducting an extensive review of literature and using theoretical analysis from the perspective of institutionalism, it is necessary to present conclusions and a short summary. **I divide the recommendations into (1) planning, (2) practical, and (3) educational ones.**

* * *

(1) **Planning activities should lead to the development of a strategy for implementing changes in public policies** responsible for civil protection. In order to build modern population protection systems, Poland, the Czech Republic and Hungary should observe both threats and good practices for overcoming them. What is particularly desirable is the development of risk analysis, which we discussed in the introductory chapter. This applies to both crises observed within the EU and the problems of the Russian-Ukrainian war. Thanks to the development of digital communication systems, modern public policy can quickly assimilate and implement changes in regulations and activities of state bodies. In addition to observation, an important element of the exchange of good practices are intergovernmental consultations, which take place in bilateral relations and in the European Union. Acquiring knowledge will allow for the outline of a precise implementation strategy.

(2) **Practical activities concern the implementation of acquired knowledge to strengthen institutions.** Countries in the Central European region need practical strategies for adapting civil protection institutions to the observed challenges. The key issue is to create a logistical base, strengthen staff and equip existing protection formations so that they can perform additional functions in the event of emergency situations. This will require additional financial outlays, which should be planned for years in advance.

(3) **Educational activities include processes of increasing the resilience** of society through media education and training. Universal security can only be achieved through the conscious participation of the population in the effort for common defense. Meanwhile, according to research, most citizens do not know what their duties are in the event of a crisis or war. Crisis training has been rare for years. Citizens must have access to information (applications, media, knowledge of supplies and protective facilities) and be aware of the existence of systems on which their security depends. A parallel challenge is the fight against disinformation, which should be the subject of a separate study.

The success of public policy in the discussed area should be considered the construction, maintenance and development of lasting institutional solutions that will create a system that (1) will maximize the efficiency of rescue services and (2) will be understandable to citizens.

References

2011. évi CXXVIII. törvény - a katasztrófavédelemről és a hozzá kapcsolódó egyes törvények módosításáról. https://civil-protection-humanitarian-aid.ec.europa.eu/system/files/2022-06/act_on_disaster_management_CXXVIII_2011_en.pdf

Act N. 320/2015 Coll. of 11 November 2015 on the Fire Rescue Service of the Czech Republic and on amendment of certain acts (Act on the Fire Rescue Service). https://ec.europa.eu/echo/files/civil_protection/national_disaster_management_system/czech_republic/320_2015_frs_cz_act.pdf

AMBRUSZ, J. *The System of Disaster Preparedness in Hungary*, in: *Educating for Democratic Governance and Global Citizenship*, World Council for Curriculum and Instruction, San Diego 2016, pp. 231–235.

Belügyminisztérium Országos Katasztrófavédelmi Főigazgatóság, 11/08/2024. https://www.katasztrofavedelem.hu/2/bemutatkozas

BOIN, A., RHINARD, M., "Crisis management performance and the European Union: the case of COVID-19", *Journal of European Public Policy*, 2023, Vol. 30, No. 4, pp. 655–675; DOI: https://doi.org/10.1080/13501763.2022.2141304

BORZILLO, L., DESCHAUX-DUTARD, D. *Secondary Analysis of Qualitative Data in Defense Studies: Methodological Opportunities and Challenges*, in: *Research Methods in Defense Studies. A Multidisciplinary Overview*, Edited by Delphine Deschaux-Dutard, Routledge, London & New York 2021, pp. 60–75. DOI: https://doi.org/10.4324/9780429198236

BRÁZOVÁ, V – K., "Response of Central European Civil Security Systems to the Economic Crisis", *Central European Journal of Public Policy*, vol. 9, no. 2, 2015, pp. 142–152. DOI: https://doi.org/10.1515/cejpp-2016-0016

Civil Protection, European Civil Protection and Humanitarian Aid Operations, European Commission. https://civil-protection-humanitarian-aid.ec.europa.eu/what/civil-protection_en

Civil protection in Hungary, June 2009. https://www.iaem.org/portals/25/documents/HungaryEM.pdf

Crisis Management Act N. 240/2000 Coll. https://ec.europa.eu/echo/files/civil_protection/national_disaster_management_system/czech_republic/239_2000_irs_cz_act.pdf

Czech Republic, European Civil Protection and Humanitarian Aid Operations. https://civil-protection-humanitarian-aid.ec.europa.eu/what/civil-protection/national-disaster-management-system/czech-republic_en

Czechia – Civil Protection, European Committee of the Regions. https://portal.cor.europa.eu/divisionpowers/Pages/Czechia-Civil-Protection.aspx

Does Poland need civil defense? February 8, 2013. https://www.nik.gov.pl/en/news/does-poland-need-civil-defence-part-1.html

European Disaster and Risk Management, European Commission. https://civil-protection-humanitarian-aid.ec.europa.eu/what/civil-protection/european-disaster-risk-management_en

FILIPEK, A. W., "Security Culture as a Challenge for Uniformed Services and Other Citizens", *Internal Security*, Vol. 12, No. 2, 2020, pp. 7–19. DOI: https://doi.org/ 10.5604/01.3001.0014.6655

First Protocol additional to the Geneva Conventions of 12 August 1949, and relating to the Protection of Victims of International Armed Conflicts, Geneva, 8 June 1977.

Government Centre for Security. https://www.gov.pl/web/rcb

Government Resolution 1163/2020 (21st April) on Hungary's National Security Strategy. https://honvedelem.hu/hirek/government-resolution-1163-2020-21st-april.html

Hatósági tevékenység ismertetése, 10/08/2024. https://www.katasztrofavedelem.hu/78/hatosagi-tevekenyseg-ismertetese

Information on the results of the audit entitled Preparation of civil defense structures to carry out tasks in times of war and peace. https://www.nik.gov.pl/en/news/nik-on-civil-defence.html;

Information on the results of the audit entitled Preparation of the system for protecting the population against natural disasters and crisis situations. https://www.nik.gov.pl/en/news/nik-on-crisis-management-2013.html

Information on the results of the audit entitled Protection of the population within the framework of crisis management and civil defense. See: Supreme Audit Office. https://www.nik.gov.pl/en/

IVANUŠA, T., PODBREGAR, I., BAKOŠ, E., BOŽEK, F., *Integrated Rescue System in the Czech Republic and in the Republic of Slovenia:*

Similarities / Differences – Advantages / Disadvantages, Conference Paper: 5th International Conference “Crisis management days”, Velika Gorica, Croatia, May 2012. https://www.researchgate.net/publication/281859686_Integrated_Rescue_System_in_the_Czech_Republic_and_in_the_Republic_of_Slovenia_Similarities_Differences_-_Advantages_Disadvantages

JAKUBIAK, E., “Coordination and Operation National Emergency And Fire System In Poland”, *National Security Studies*, vol. 18, 2020, pp. 35–43. DOI: https://doi.org/10.37055/sbn/145295

KALINOWSKI, R., *Obrona Cywilna w Polsce*, Uniwersytet w Siedlcach, Siedlce 2017.

KAVAN, S., “Provisions of Civil Defence Training in Czechoslovakia – Historical Consequences”, *Security Dimensions*, vol. 47, 2024, pp. 44–58. DOI: https://doi.org/10.5604/01.3001.0054.6713

KOWALKOWSKI, S., WRZOSEK, M., KAŹMIERCZAK, D., “Challenges to Civil Protection in Times of Future Wars”, *Wiedza Obronna*, vol. 284, no. 3, 2023. DOI: https://doi.org/10.34752/2023-a284

KOMPAN, J., HRNČIAR, M., “The Security Sector Reform of the Fragile State as a Tool for Conflict Prevention”, *Politické Vedy*, Vol. 24, No. 2, 2021 pp. 87–107. DOI: https://doi.org/ 10.24040/politickevedy.2021.24.2.87-107

KOPCZEWSKI, M., SZMITKOWSKI, P., “Civil Defense In Poland – Transformation Process After 1989. Current State And Modernization Proposals”, *De Securitate et Defensione*, No. 1 (6) 2020, pp. 75–87. DOI: https://doi.org/10.34739/dsd.2020.01.04

KOZÁRI, L., *System of Hungarian System Management*, Defense Technical Information Center Compilation Part Notice, ADP013436 (Unclassified). https://apps.dtic.mil/sti/tr/pdf/ADP013436.pdf

KRZYKOWSKI, P., “Defense Infrastructure - an Attempt at Identification”, *Security and Defense Quarterly*, vol. 22, 2018, pp. 71–98. DOI: https://doi.org/10.5604/01.3001.0012.7589

KUNIKOWSKI, G., ROSTEK, K., “Good practices in civil planning and crisis management in the world and their implementation in Poland”, *Jagiellonian Journal of Management*, vol. 3 (2017), no. 3, pp. 135–150. DOI: https://doi.org/10.4467/2450114XJJM.17.009.9560

MALEŠIČ, M., "The Union Civil Protection Mechanism in the Prism of Solidarity Theory", *Journal of Comparative Politics*, vol. 18, no. 1, 2025, pp. 34–50.

MARCH, J.G., OLSEN, J.P., "The New Institutionalism: Organizational Factors in Political Life", *The American Political Science Review*, Vol. 78, No. 3 (Sep., 1984), pp. 734–749. DOI: https://doi.org/10.2307/1961840

National Security Council, Government of the Czech Republic. https://vlada.gov.cz/en/ppov/brs/office-of-the-government-of-the-czech-republic-23851/

NOVAKY, M., KATAI-URBAN, L., "Development of Civil Protection in Hungary", *Зарубежный опыт: гражданская защита*, pp. 89–95. DOI: https://doi.org/10.25257/FE.2018.1.89-95 https://cyberleninka.ru/article/n/development-of-civil-protection-in-hungary

NOVAKY, M., "Hungary's Disaster Management Tasks in the Light of the Challenges of Defense and Security in the 21st Century", *Security Dimensions*, no. 42, 2022, pp. 36–47. DOI: https://doi.org/10.5604/01.3001.0016.0734

OSTROWSKA, R., "Civil defense in Poland from a historical perspective", *Scientific Journal of the Military University of Land Forces*, 2021, Volume 53, Number 3 (201), pp. 496–506. DOI: https://doi.org/10.5604/01.3001.0015.3402

PARKER, Ch., PERSSON, T., WIDMALM, S., "The Effectiveness of National and EU-level Civil Protection Systems: Evidence from 17 Member States", *Journal of European Public Policy*, vol. 26, issue 9, 2019, pp. 1312–1334. https://doi.org/10.1080/13501763.2018.1523219

PAWŁUSZKO, T., *Civil Protection in Poland and Hungary. Searching for good practices*, Sobieski Institute, 12 August 2024. https://sobieski.org.pl/en/civil-protection-in-poland-and-hungary-searching-for-good-practices/

PAWŁUSZKO, T., "Crisis of Civil Defense in Poland. Institutional Perspective", *National Security Studies*, vol. 30, 4/2023, pp. 41–62. DOI: https://doi.org/10.37055/sbn/175516

PETKOV, V., TAGAREV, T., "Hungary: Capabilities, Organizations, Policies, and Legislation in crisis management and disaster response", *Connections. The Quarterly Journal*, ITSec4 Reports 127, Sofia, March 2015. https://connections-qj.org/article/hungary-capabilities-organizations-policies-and-legislation-crisis-management-and-disaster

PIETREK, G., "The crisis management system and the civil protection system. Similarities, differences, possibilities of standardization", *Security and Defense Quarterly*, vol. 16, no. 3/2017, pp. 75–88. DOI: https://doi.org/10.35467/sdq/103185

PIOTROWSKA-MICHALAK, J. "Defence tasks carried out by local governments in Poland", *De Securitate et Defensione*, 2 (6) 2020, pp. 185–204. DOI: https://doi.org/10.34739/dsd.2020.02.13

Poland introduces "landmark" new civil defense law, Notes from Poland, December 19, 2024. https://notesfrompoland.com/2024/12/19/poland-introduces-landmark-new-civil-defence-law/

PREBILIČ, V., "Crisis Management in Municipality: The Role Of Civil Protection During Covid-19 Crisis", *Journal of Comparative Politics*, vol. 15, no. 1, 2022, pp. 56–72.

Resilience in NATO, December 15, 2023. https://www.act.nato.int/article/resilience-in-nato/

SKRABACZ, A., PAJKA, A., WIĘCKOWSKI, B., "Crisis Management as a Research Province of Security Science", *Roczniki Nauk Społecznych*, vol. 16, no. 1, 2024, pp. 7–25. DOI: https://doi.org/10.18290/rns2024.0010

SOBOLEWSKI, G., "Systemic Approach to Civil Protection in Poland", *Safety and Fire Technology*, vol. 54 (2), 2019, pp. 116–131. https://www.doi.org/10.12845/sft.54.2.2019.9

SZYNOWSKI, R., ŠČUREK, R., "Crisis Management in Public Administration Units in Poland and Czech Republic. International Comparative Analysis", *Internal Security*, vol. 16, no. 1, 2024, pp. 59–82. DOI: https://doi.org/10.5604/01.3001.0054.7093

TEKNŐS, L., "Analysis and Assessment of the Growing Tendencies of Natural Disasters and Events in Hungary from the Perspective of Disaster Management", *Security Dimensions*, vol. 43, no. 43, 2022, pp. 53–75. DOI: https://doi.org/10.5604/01.3001.0054.1483

The national disaster management system, European Commission. https://civil-protection-humanitarian-aid.ec.europa.eu/what/civil-protection/national-disaster-management-system_en

The Structure, Role and Mandate of Civil Protection in Disaster Risk Reduction for South Eastern Europe South Eastern Europe Disaster Risk Mitigation and Adaptation Program, United Nations Office for the Coordination of

Humanitarian Affairs (OCHA), Emergency Preparedness Section Palais des Nations, Geneva 2009. https://www.undrr.org/publication/structure-role-and-mandate-civil-protection-disaster-risk-reduction-south-eastern

TURSKA-KAWA, A., CSANYI, P., KUCHARČÍK, R., "From the "Rally 'Round The Flag" Effect to a Social Crisis of Confidence. Poland and Slovakia in the First Year of the Covid-19 Pandemic", *Journal of Comparative Politics*, vol. 15, no. 1, 2022, pp. 20–38.

Ukraine report, European Commission. https://civil-protection-humanitarian-aid.ec.europa.eu/where/europe/ukraine_en

Ukrainian Refugees and Migrants in the German Labour Market. Preliminary Research Results

Robert Geisler[69]

ABSTRACT
The aim of the paper is to analyze the refugees and war migration among Ukrainians in the German labour market. Based on qualitative and quantitative research, the results of the research are the following: lack of integration in the German labour market and German society among refugees and migrants, lack of willingness to pursue education or language skills improvement, and different attitudes among German entrepreneurs from support to anxiety. However, there is need for labour force in the German labour market, and any successful programs or training towards Ukrainian citizens were provided. In conclusion, German labour market policy should take into consideration Ukrainian citizens' attitudes and values in relation to creating new programs for integration.

Keywords: refugees, migrants, integration, labour market, Ukraine

Introduction

Catastrophic disasters and wars represent profound crises that challenge both governance and societal resilience. From the social sciences perspective, these crises often change the governance systems, political-decision making, public policies and legitimacy. Disruption of governance, risk, unstable regulations, and a lack of trust towards institutions create special challenges for political leaders. Russian aggression towards Ukraine in February 2022 was one of the important events that destroyed the political order in Europe but also destabilized labour markets and everyday activities of European governments, companies and citizens. In November 2023, 4.2 million Ukrainians used the mechanism of temporary protection in the EU countries, among them 1 235 960 in Germany, 955 110 in Poland, and 396 330 in The Czech Republic.

The aims of the paper will be to present preliminary research results regarding the integration of Ukrainian refugees and migrants into the German labour market and, in a broad sense, German society in 2024 – two years

69 Robert Geisler - University of Opole, Associate Professor, The Chair of the Governance and Public Policy Department. https://orcid.org/0000-0002-0218-980X

after the aggression. The main research question was to analyze the human capital of Ukrainian refugees and migrants /their language skills, competences, expectations, future plans, aspirations/.

During the research, the following research methods were used: 1) A survey, regarding the attitudes of Ukrainian refugees and migrants, expectations analysis; and the attitudes and expectations of German entrepreneurs regarding opportunities for refugees/migrants' employment. 2) An Individual Deep Interview (IDI) realized with stakeholders of the project, which means experts from state organizations and NGO's working on the integration of the Ukrainian migrants with the German labour market[70].

State-of-the art

The integration of migrants and refugees into receiving societies remains a challenge that intersects with economic, social, cultural and political dimensions[71]. Recent scholarship has increasingly emphasized the concept

[70] The qualitative study – IDI methods were conducted in the group of 10 respondents – experts, who are working on the field of integration and adaptation of migrants/refugees with German Society. In the qualitative research part - a total of 58 entrepreneurs took part in the survey, with 25% women and 65% men and 8% of the unspecified sex. In terms of age, entrepreneurs in the 26–35 age group dominated (48% of respondents), followed by 27% of respondents aged 36–45. In terms of business size, respondents from medium-sized enterprises dominated and accounted for 63% of respondents, compared to 27% of respondents from small enterprises and only 8.6% from large enterprises. In terms of place of business, one in five respondents had their company located in Berlin, 17% in Hamburg, 13% in Stuttgart and individuals from other cities such as Aachen, Dresden, Hannover, Munich, Leipzig, Nuernberg. The respondents represented the following industries: business, financial services, manufacturing, research and development, trade, medical, i.e. a very wide range of economic sectors. A total of 118 respondents – migrants and refugees took part in the survey, 66% of whom were women and 28% men, which roughly corresponds to the general population of Ukrainian refugees in Germany. In terms of age, respondents in the 35–44 age group dominated the survey and accounted for one third of the survey population. One in four respondents was under the age of 24 and 22% were aged 25–34. In terms of education, those with vocational or secondary education predominated. The description of the research sample shows the Ukrainian refugee as predominantly a young or middle-aged woman (half of the respondents are under 44 years of age) with no higher education.

[71] H. Crawley & D. Skleparis, "Refugees, Migrants, Neither Both", *Journal of Ethnic and Migrant Studies*, 4, 2018, pp. 48–64. https://doi.org/10.1080/1369183X.2017.1348224

of *multi-level governance* in integration policies, highlighting the roles of national, regional, and local authorities, as well as civil society organizations, in facilitating integration pathways[72]. Economically, labour market integration is identified as a cornerstone of successful adaptation, with studies underscoring the importance of language acquisition, skills recognition, and anti-discrimination measures in reducing barriers to employment. Social and cultural integration, meanwhile, focuses on fostering social cohesion through community-based initiatives, intercultural dialogue, and inclusive education systems[73]. Another issue is building entrepreneurship attitudes and companies by refugees and migrants[74]. In this case the question is, how migrants are supported by eco-system or in which way they are so active and strong that are able to use legal system, their language skills and circumstances to create company or be independent as freelancer or employer.

The global refugee crisis in 2014–2015 resulted in the migration of millions of refugees to the EU countries, including some 890,000 refugees to Germany[75]. The structures built to help refugees, and the financial resources allocated for this purpose have yielded results of various kinds: from the integration of some people who have found employment or graduated from schools, including higher education, to people still living, i.e. in 2024, in deprived neighborhoods, without work and often in conflict with the law. As a result of the above experiences, the issue of integrating refugees into the German labour market is becoming a key challenge not only for public policies, but also for entrepreneurs who are struggling to find resources for work.

Russia's aggression against Ukraine in 2022 replicated, in a way, this situation from a few years ago. The arrival of approximately 1 million Ukrainian refugees in Germany within the first 18 months following the Russian invasion - predominantly women and children - resulted in increased humanitarian

---

72 N. Zaun, *EU Asylum Policies*. Palgrave Macmillan, London & New York 2017.

73 D. della Porta (ed), *Solidarity Mobilizations in the 'Refugee Crisis'. Contentious Moves*. Palgrave Macmillan, London & New York 2018.

74 G. Zalkat, H. Barth, L. Rashid, "Refugee Entrepreneurship motivations in Sweden and Germany: A comparative Study", *Small Business Economics*, Vol. 63, 2024, No 4, pp. 477–499.

75 C. T. Schmidt, "Germany's „Open Door" Policy in Light of the Recent Refugees Crises. AN Interpretive Reasons and Underlying Motivations". Linkoeping University. Master Thesis. Linkoeping 2016.

activity by German society. Almost two years after the problem arose, as of 30.11.2023, there were almost 1 157 000 Ukrainian citizens in Germany, some of whom intend to settle and stay permanently[76].

The German entrepreneurial perspective qualitative research results

How, therefore, to integrate migrants and refugees in case of employment, a place to live, or a broadly defined living space? The results of qualitative research conducted among experts, i.e. people involved in the integration of migrants and refugees, and business supporters show an interesting broad phenomenon. Firstly, it is important to start - according to the respondents - with defining the term 'integration', a concept that experts believe is vague. Does integration refer solely to a migrant's self-reliance in the labour market or healthcare systems, or does it encompass a more fundamental sense of self-sufficiency? Here, the experts agreed on the first understanding of the term, integration means self-reliance. Secondly, based on their experience and observation, the experts divided the migrants into three groups: the first one consisted of very active people, with a decision to stay in Germany, and a desire to find employment, i.e. highly motivated to integrate into the German labour market. The second group is made up of people aged 50+ who have difficulties communicating in German, often have diplomas not recognized by German employers, and the degree of adaptation to German society is more complex. The third group includes people who are not motivated to remain in German society, passive in their adaptation behaviour, but at the same time intend to benefit from the German welfare system.

These are mostly people waiting for the end of the war conflict within Ukraine. Thirdly, it is worth pointing out the attitudes of entrepreneurs. In the early months, a humanitarian approach was clearly evident, with broad-ranging support provided to war refugees. In the following months, they began to reflect on the cost of such an undertaking. In an even broader perspective, it is possible to talk about the cost of public spending, i.e. a macro approach, in which the cost of helping refugees is one of the important issues,

---

[76] *Annual Report on Migration and Asylum 2022. Statistical Annex*. Co-produced by Eurostat and the European Migration Network. June 2023.

and the source of this cost can be found, inter alia, in taxes on businesses and entrepreneurs.

Although it must be noted that for many entrepreneurs, refugees and migrants were a marginal issue. They were focused on their business activities at all times, and when it came to hiring employees, who are in short supply on the German market, the secondary issue was their origin, whether they were German citizens or foreigners. The idea of humanitarian entrepreneurial assistance in the spirit of corporate social responsibility has been superseded by a pragmatic approach, i.e. the need to employ workers. The lack of German language skills was one of the key barriers to employing refugees from Ukraine. In turn, this barrier was difficult to overcome due to, among other things, the lack of German language teachers and the possibility to provide language courses for them. As the experts pointed out in the macrostructural approach, a holistic approach is needed, which assumes the active participation of entrepreneurs in the implementation of the refugee/migrant integration process, consisting of programmes combining inclusion in individual jobs together with German language training.

The level of human capital of refugees and migrants

The survey conducted with Ukrainian migrants and refugees started with a very general question about the skills needed in German companies. The employers surveyed indicated, on the one hand, those related to the specifics of the industry such as the ability to drive trucks, competences in the medical industry - nursing, physiotherapy, accounting, work experience. On the other hand, there are universal competences concerning employees, such as education, language skills, communication skills, teamwork, leadership, adaptation to change, flexibility, emotional intelligence, critical thinking, the ability to use social media, and problem solving.

It is interesting to note that employers surveyed were more likely to indicate universal qualities than specific professional qualities. General qualities are more in demand than specific learned qualities, which is a facilitator for hiring migrants. On the other hand, however, cultural differences can often be an obstacle to German employers and migrants defining universal qualities in the same way.

Cultural differences also play a significant role in the labour market. In this open-ended question, in their answers, entrepreneurs pointed to opportunities for the development of their companies, but also to the culture shock that came to them in direct contact with people from a different culture. A small percentage of responses referred to becoming aware of difficulties, but also to reflecting on the phenomenon of being able to overcome them and use them as a resource for work. The survey asked respondents whether they had ever employed refugees. The vast majority of the survey - 62% - said yes, and a further 17% said they had done so at least once, showing that 4/5 of the respondents had experience employing refugees. This may also be related to the fact that the majority of respondents in the survey were those who have this kind of experience. In other words, entrepreneurs with experience in employing foreigners applied for the survey. This relates to specific industries - cf. labour market analysis.

Of those who hired foreigners, 58% of those surveyed, the vast majority, felt neither fear nor apprehension about hiring a non-German, although a third of those surveyed admitted to feeling fear at the beginning of the recruitment process, and only 12% of those surveyed said they had no feelings about it.

Among those employing foreigners, entrepreneurs with experience with employees from Asian countries dominated with 67% and 12% from Ukraine. This is due to the fact that, since there has been a refugee crisis in Europe for about 10 years, many people from Asian countries have found their way to Germany and found employment in German companies in the following years. As the issue of Ukrainian refugees is a relatively new one, this has an impact on their low employment to date. Almost one-third of the respondents provided support to employed foreigners to almost 70% of entrepreneurs who did not. The vast majority of entrepreneurs did not take any steps to integrate refugees into German society or the German labour market. Of those who did provide support, 81% indicated a German language course, and 35% suggested the pursuit of some type of additional vocational qualification.

How do employers assess the role of public institutions in integrating refugees into the German labour market? - was another important question asked in the online survey. The highest number of indications, 77%, concerned financial support for targeted projects aimed at refugees as direct beneficiaries of these projects. On the other hand, 55% and 56% of the indications were related to financial support for entrepreneurs, e.g. tax breaks and support for refugees in organising German language courses and training courses for them to confirm/complete their existing qualifications.

As many as 75% of respondents see benefits for themselves in the employment of refugees/migrants, compared to 25% of respondents who do not. Among the benefits, the entrepreneurs surveyed cited help for entrepreneurs and new insights into the processes involved. On the other hand, for a quarter of the respondents who stated that employment has no benefits for them, they cited language problems, the lack of trust, and the lack of experience.

The second survey was realized with Ukrainian migrants and refugees. At the outset, respondents were asked which professions or industries they were most interested in for their future work. In answering this question, respondents expressed, on the one hand, expectations related to their education and qualifications—such as becoming an accountant, HR specialist, marketing specialist, doctor, IT specialist, engineer, journalist, lawyer, actor, nurse, psychologist, or therapist. A whole list of different types of professions appeared, without any clearly dominant one, which is a reflection of the professional structure of people migrating from Ukraine to Germany. On the other hand, there were answers concerning such activities or jobs as cleaning rooms, creative professions, and construction, which were indicated by respondents with lower education. A review of the responses indicates the existence among the surveyed Ukrainian migrants of relatively high competences and qualifications acquired in their country of origin and the lack of such competences. This allows a conclusion to be drawn about the stratification of the migrant group into two subgroups. It therefore becomes important to make use of existing competences in the German labour market and to select people with these competences beforehand.

Do you have experience with German companies? - The distribution of answers to the question phrased in this way was as follows: 51% of respondents indicated that they did not, compared to 48% positive responses. Respondents form two fairly equal groups of those with and without experience with German companies. There is still self-alienation or segregation in the labour market. For those with positive experiences in the labour market, the question was asked how they found a job. A small number of answers emerged here - via the internet or online. This clearly shows the role of new technologies in the integration of refugees and its use by those concerned themselves.

An indicator of labour market activity is the search for work by the unemployed. The situation is analogous to refugees and migrants from Ukraine. It is therefore interesting and noteworthy that 53% of respondents indicated that they are looking for work. In contrast, 46% of respondents answered negatively to this question, which means that every second person surveyed is not looking for a job, i.e. remains passive on the German labour market. Of those who were active, those aged 35–44 and under 24 were the most active. Those between 25–34 very often explained having school-age children, which prevented them from being active on the labour market. Those declaring a positive answer were asked an additional question about where they looked for work. The predominant answer was the internet – 63%, friends – 13%, and activity centers – 11%. This confirms previous responses about the role of technology in the social integration of refugees and the role of technology in the transmission of information and knowledge about the labour market.

From the perspective of the refugee integration project, it is important to understand the reasons for inactivity in the labour market. Individual responses from respondents indicated a lack of motivation for having children. The lack of responses, on the other hand, clearly suggests a strong sense of passivity among respondents. A practical issue to be addressed is to build motivation and a sense of purpose among refugees and to provide childcare for mothers/young women.

The future of respondents, which means their projection, attitudes and expectations towards the next years of living, was one of the fundamental issues. So, the question was - Do you intend to look for work? One in two respondents indicated a positive answer, while 28% of respondents declared that they did not, and one in five indicated that it was 'difficult to say'. On the one hand, almost half of the respondents declare themselves to be active on the labour market, on the other hand, an almost equal group of "relative passives", in other words, not very convinced of their activity, deserves attention. Throughout the survey, one can notice a division of the surveyed population into two more or less equal groups - active on the labour market and passive. This division runs along age lines - the older people are, the more they are convinced that they have fewer opportunities on the labour market.

Table 1: Survey question about seeking employment on the German labour market

Cross-Table Did you looking for a job on the German labour market? And are you able to look for a job on the labour market?					
		Are you able to look for a job on the labour market?			
		Difficult to say	**No**	**Yes**	**Sum**
Did you look for a job on the German labour market?	No	15	34	6	55
	Yes	9	0	54	63
Sum		24	34	60	118

The table above shows a strong relationship between the two analysed variables. Those who are active and have already looked for a job in the German labour market intend to find their place in it. They are determined, have a sense of agency, and maintain a conviction of achieving their goal. In other words, a sense of activity translates into a sense of agency and consequently finding a place of employment.

The vast majority of respondents, 82%, agreed with the statement that they would use an app to help and facilitate their stay in Germany and gather information on official matters. From the point of view of labour market integration, issues of retraining and training are important. Only 33% of respondents declared that they have been able to participate in training so far, against two-thirds who are deprived of such opportunities, according to their opinion. This is a significant finding for those designing integration processes – how to reach a group of employees and what training opportunities to offer them. A single positive vote concerned participation in a German language course.

What qualifications do you need to find a job on the German market? - is another question /open-ended/, to which the respondents answered as follows:

- Adaptation to the German labour market, to the culture;
- Education, recognition of qualifications and diplomas;
- German language skills;
- Work experience.

With the aim of integrating refugees/migrants into the German labour market, such a process cannot do without knowledge of German, the primary language of communication in the labour market. When assessing their language competences, migrants from Ukraine declared that 39% of the sample indicated their knowledge of German at the B1 level, 28% at the A2 level, 15% at the A1 level, and only one in ten at the B2 level. The results of this kind of survey show relatively low language competences, which need to be strengthened and improved in order to be able to talk about the integration of these people into the labour market.

The respondents were then asked to respond to several statements aimed at diagnosing their career aspirations and attitudes towards working and living in Germany. The first was a statement regarding intentions to stay in Germany and find a job. The results are somewhat surprising, as almost a third responded negatively to this type of statement, i.e. they are those intending to return to Ukraine or move to another country. A positive response was given by more than 45% of the respondents - “definitely yes” and “rather yes” (4 and 5) answers.

Table 2: Survey question about the decision to look for a job in Germany

11a. I am going to stay in Germany and find a job			
		N	%
Criteria	1	35	29,7
	2	20	16,9
	3	10	8,5
	4	31	26,3
	5	22	18,6
	Sum	118	100,0

The second indicator was the knowledge of legal issues concerning job searching and employment in Germany. As many as 88% of respondents expressed a negative opinion, i.e. a lack of knowledge of legal issues concerning employment on the German labour market.

Table 3: Survey question about knowledge of legal working conditions in Germany

11b. I know legal issues to find a job in Germany			
		N	%
Criteria	1	71	60,2
	2	33	28,0
	3	6	5,1
	4	6	5,1
	5	2	1,7
	Sum	118	100,0

Another indicator was the respondents' knowledge of legal issues related to working in Germany. Analogous to the previous question, 80% of respondents have no knowledge in this area. The answer to the next question confirms the same attitude and knowledge of refugees, as 79% of respondents believe that they need help and support with legal issues in the labour market. The answer to the next question, concerning the role of social networks, is interesting. Based on respondents' declarations, a picture emerges of refugees as members of a highly individualised society or without social networks with participants in the German labour market, as 86 % of respondents answered negatively to the question that family and friends play an important role in finding a job. A picture emerges of refugees as relatively lonely, abandoned and left to their own devices. In support of this, the answers to another question can be cited, where 78% of respondents indicated that family members and friends did not support them in finding a job in Germany.

The validity of the above thesis is confirmed by the fact that 80% of the respondents were of the opinion that they do not have many friends among German workers, which supports the thesis of the relative social isolation of refugees/migrants.

Another interesting indicator is the declaration of respondents (80% of indications) that they have sufficient qualifications and skills to take up employment in Germany. Refugees express confidence in their qualifications, which, in combination with a low level of German language skills and education, allows the conclusion to be drawn about the need for further training or retraining with a high degree of self-confidence. In a further statement relating to the feeling of conviction that migrants will find employment on the German market, as many as 42% expressed such conviction, compared to 39% of respondents with the opposite opinion. The values of the answers to the above question are fairly evenly distributed.

On the other hand, as many as 90% of the respondents expressed the belief that it is important for them to find a job matching their qualifications and competences. It is noteworthy that often migrants or refugees start their working lives in a new country with jobs below their previous qualifications and competences.

We will summarize the descriptive statistics of the responses to the above questions. Of all the statements, the predominant beliefs among respondents are the importance of finding a job in line with their qualifications and competences, the sufficiency of these qualifications and competences, and the need for support in terms of knowledge of the law.

Table 4: Statistical analysis of survey responses

Descriptive Statistics			
	Average	Standard Deviation	N
11a. I am going to stay in Germany and find a job	2,87	1,539	118
11b. I know the legal requirements for finding a job in Germany	1,60	,926	118
11c. I know legal issues regarding work in Germany	1,73	1,067	118
11d. I need support in legal issues while looking for a job in Germany	4,25	1,117	118
11e. My friends play key role in finding a job in Germany	1,85	1,217	118
11f. I have a lot of friends among German workers.	1,81	1,139	118
11g. My qualifications and skills are enough to find a job in Germany.	4,25	1,176	118
11h. I am sure to find a job in Germany.	3,05	1,313	118
11i. It is important for me to find a job related to my qualifications and skills.	4,55	1,975	118

Figure 1: Migrant's Opinion about their Skills and Future.
Source: own study.

An interesting issue was to present the opinions of migrants related to their expectations to German entrepreneurs. More than 70% of answers found that they expect special treatment, and then a long-term period of adaptation.

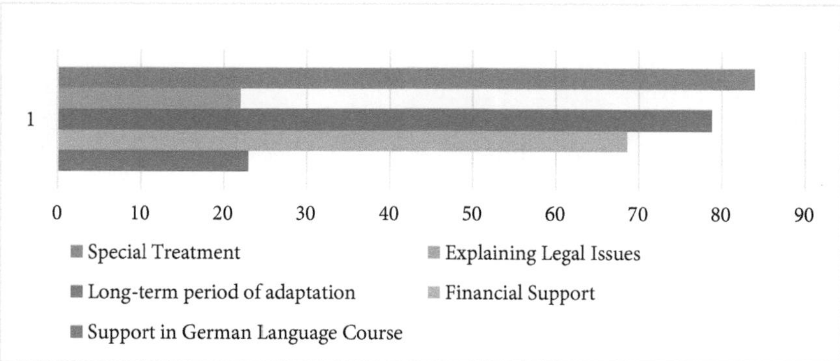

Figure 2: What do you expect from German entrepreneurs?
Source: own study.

Summarizing the results of the survey research, it can be concluded that the surveyed migrants and refugees are two more or less equal groups: on the one hand, active in the market and society and positive, and on the other hand, passive and passive. They commonly share characteristics such as limited German language skills, social isolation, and often a lack of qualifications recognized by the German labour market. Additionally, they frequently lack support from family and friends, as well as knowledge of legal and administrative matters related to residence in Germany or the EU. Differences between members of the two refugee population groups are the degree of activity on the labour market, the conviction of finding a job among German companies and the motivation to work.

Surveys indicate that the main dividing line is age - young people under 24 and those aged 35–44, i.e. those with slightly older children, have more language skills and more conviction in finding a job. Those with young children are characterised by passivity and apathy, explaining having children and having to care for them prevents them from entering the labour market.

Conclusions

The conclusions of the quantitative survey of German entrepreneurs yielded several key conclusions: Firstly, a significant barrier to employment is, in the opinion of the entrepreneurs surveyed, the insufficient knowledge of the German language by migrants/refugees from Ukraine. The day-to-day running of the job also requires extensive intercultural communication, i.e. an understanding of cultural differences by employers and employees. This means an emphasis on German language training, followed by the training of competences and qualifications needed by individual companies. At the same time, this kind of practice can be combined, i.e. language courses can be implemented with everyday work practice. Secondly, it is worth considering building up trust in refugees, as, so far, a lack of trust and sometimes even fear of employment or direct contact with migrants prevail. This issue was also pointed out by employers who already have experience with employing foreigners. Thirdly, it is worth considering the participation of refugees in internship or apprenticeship projects aimed at establishing direct contact with entrepreneurs who employ or have already employed refugees/migrants. It is significant that the entrepreneurs mentioned have already gone through an evolution of thinking from fear /nearly one-third of the respondents/ to the acceptance of this state of affairs. Fourthly, the experiences gained from employing migrants between 2014 and 2020—mainly from Asian countries—could be utilized, for example, by promoting good practices in the labour market. Fifthly, the need to diagnose the needed competences in German companies in the context of their supply by migrants and to educate the needed competences and qualifications among migrants/refugees has become apparent. Therefore, there is a need for support from public institutions, first and foremost in the area of German language training and in the further acquisition of competences among migrants/refugees, but nevertheless direct allocation of resources to those interested in participating in such an endeavor is indicated. One may also wonder to what extent the costs of the mentioned projects will also be borne by entrepreneurs. On the other hand, the question arises: how to interest beneficiaries in participating in this kind of undertaking, and how to identify the interested people themselves?

Quantitative and qualitative research on the opinions and declarations about the integration of refugees and migrants from Ukraine into the German labour market leads to some fundamental conclusions. Integration means, first and foremost, independence, i.e. moving into a social and physical space without any assistance. This can be achieved, above all, with the basic prerequisite of knowledge of the German language. At present there is a relatively low level of knowledge of the German language in the context of employment and working life and a low level of knowledge of the legal aspects of working life. Therefore, there is a need for knowledge of the German language, a relatively advanced use of the language and knowledge of the legal issues of finding oneself in German society.

It is clear from the research that the use of technology allows the use of an integration app as one of the important tools. Such an app should be easy to use and contain knowledge and information about legal issues, health care, or the labour market. The app in question can have inbuilt German language teaching functions. In addition, coaching, psychological functions such as online courses, webinars on motivation or intercultural differences are indicated. Furthermore, the app can also function as a Hub, i.e. a space for connecting businesses and active refugees, a referral system for employees and companies/jobs.

References

Annual Report on Migration and Asylum 2022. Statistical Annex. Co-produced by Eurostat and the European Migration Network. June 2023.

CRAWLEY, H., & SKLEPARIS, D., "Refugees, Migrants, Neither Both", *Journal of Ethnic and Migrant Studies*, 4, 2018, 48–64. https://doi.org/10.1080/1369183X.2017.1348224

PORTA DELLA D. (ed) *Solidarity Mobilizations in the 'Refugee Crisis'. Contentious Moves*. Palgrave Macmillan, London & New York 2018.

SCHMIDT C. T., *Germany's "Open Door" Policy in Light of the Recent Refugees Crises. AN Interpretive Reasons and Underlying Motivations*. Linkoeping University. Master Thesis, 2016.

ZALKAT G., BARTH H., RASHID L., "Refugee Entrepreneurship motivations in Sweden and Germany: A comparative Study", *Small Business Economics*, Vol. 63, No 4, 2024, pp. 477–499.

ZAUN, N., *EU Asylum Policies*, Palgrave Macmillan, London & New York 2024.

Cooperation of Emergency Services in the Face of Flood Threats: The Case of the Opolskie Province

Bartosz Maziarz[77]

ABSTRACT
This chapter analyzes the crucial role of cooperation between the State Fire Service (PSP), the Police, and the Opolskie Center for Medical Rescue in mass threat situations such as floods. Using the Opolskie Voivodeship as a case study, this publication demonstrates how effective collaboration among these services can significantly mitigate the impacts of natural disasters and protect the lives and property of citizens. Additionally, the book examines public policies that support and enhance such cooperation.

Keywords: flood, police, safety, fire service, crisis management

Introduction

Located in southwestern Poland, the Opolskie Province is a region that, despite its small area, faces a variety of natural hazards, including floods. In the context of climate change, which causes an intensification of meteorological phenomena, the cooperation of emergency services is becoming a key element of effective crisis management. This text aims to examine the mechanisms of cooperation among various institutions responsible for responding to flood risks in the Opolskie Province, as well as to assess their effectiveness and identify areas requiring improvement. In the face of flood risks, the cooperation of emergency services is a key element of effective crisis management. In the case of the Opolskie Province, which is exposed to a variety of flood-related threats, understanding the dynamics of cooperation among different rescue agencies and other stakeholders is essential to ensure an effective response to crisis situations. This cooperation extends to not only government institutions but also non-governmental organisations and local communities, which play an important role in the crisis management process. In studies devoted to flood risk management, a key aspect is to

[77] Bartosz Maziarz - University of Opole, Assistant Professor, Department of Governance and Public Policy, ORCID: https://orcid.org/0000-0002-2190-7969

analyse the intensity of cooperation among different actors. Dostál, Heijer, et al. emphasise that effective management of flood defence resources requires cooperation, which can be shaped by different intensities of cooperation[78]. In the context of the Opolskie Province, where there are different levels of flood risks, an understanding of these intensities can help to better adapt disaster management strategies to local conditions. An important element of cooperation is also taking into account the changing social and environmental conditions that affect the public's vulnerability to flooding. Klijn et al. point out that flood risk management policies in the Netherlands did not take into full consideration increasing social vulnerability, with a consequent underestimation of risk[79]. In the context of the Opole region, similar phenomena may occur, highlighting the need for regular evaluation and adaptation of crisis management policies to changing conditions. Also in their research on the availability of emergency services in the face of floods, Yang et al. point out the need to consider different disaster scenarios, such as fluvial floods, in planning the location of rescue facilities[80]. In the case of the Opolskie Province, which can be exposed to different types of floods, it is crucial that evacuation plans and the location of rescue services be adapted to the specific geographical and hydrological conditions.

---

[78] F. Heijer, J. Rijke, M. Bosch-Rekveldt, A., M. Leeuw, M. Barciela-Rial, "Asset management of flood defences as a co-production — an analysis of cooperation in five situations in the Netherlands", *Journal of Flood Risk Management*, 16(3), 2023. https://doi.org/10.1111/jfr3.12909 and J. Dostál, "Lessons of cooperation between government and non-governmental organizations in emergency management in the Czech Republic", *International Journal of Safety and Security Engineering*, 5(3), 2015, pp. 203–221. https://doi.org/10.2495/safe-v5-n3-203-221

[79] F. Klijn, K. Bruijn, J. Knoop, J. Kwadijk, "Assessment of the Netherlands' flood risk management policy under global change", *Ambio*, 41(2), 2011, pp. 180–192. https://doi.org/10.1007/s13280-011-0193-x; Q. Wang, Y. Bai & Y. Yang, "The Stackelberg game model of cross-border river flood control", *Frontiers in Ecology and Evolution*, 10, 2022. https://doi.org/10.3389/fevo.2022.964679; R. Wilby, R. Keenan, "Adapting to flood risk under climate change", *Progress in Physical Geography Earth and Environment*, 36(3), 2012, pp. 348–378. https://doi.org/10.1177/0309133312438908

[80] Y. Yang, J. Yin, M. Ye, D. She, J. & Yu, "Multi-coverage optimal location model for Emergency Medical Service (EMS) facilities under various disaster scenarios: a case study of urban fluvial floods in the Minhang District of Shanghai, China". *Natural Hazards and Earth System Science*, 20(1), 2020, pp. 181–195. https://doi.org/10.5194/nhess-20-181-2020

Geographical and hydrological context

The Opolskie Province is characterised by a diverse landscape, dominated by lowland areas and the valleys of such major rivers as the Odra, Mała Panew, and Nysa Kłodzka rivers and their drainage basins. These geographical conditions make the region particularly vulnerable to flooding, especially during periods of heavy rainfall. It is worth noting that climate change leads to more frequent and more intense rainfall, which in turn increases the risk of flooding. Therefore, understanding the local hydrological conditions is crucial for effective emergency planning.

Crisis situation planning and preparation process

In the context of flood risks, the process of planning and preparing for possible crisis situations plays a fundamental role. In the Opolskie Province, crisis management plans are developed as part of preventive measures, which take into account, among other things, hydrological forecasts, hazard maps, and evacuation procedures. Cooperation among various services is essential during the development of these plans to ensure their comprehensiveness and effectiveness. Regular emergency drills and simulations are an important part of preparation activities, enabling rescue services to hone their skills and identify any gaps in the system.

Planning and preparing for crisis situations, particularly in the context of flood risks, is a key element of risk management. In the case of the Opolskie Province, this process requires an integrated approach that takes into account both technical and social aspects. The literature on the subject, including the publications by Bernard Wiśniewski[81], emphasises the importance of a holistic approach to flood risk management, which includes both prevention and response to crisis situations.

The first step in the planning process is a thorough flood risk analysis. In this context, it is crucial to understand local hydrological conditions and to identify the areas most vulnerable to flooding. It is worth noting the need to

---

81 B. Wiśniewski, G. S. Sander, "Threat, crisis and critical situation – contemporary determinants of modern man's living conditions", *Bezpieczeństwo i Technika Pożarnicza*, (41), 2016, pp. 13–18. https://doi.org/10.12845/bitp.41.1.2016.1 and B. Wiśniewski, B. Kaczmarczyk, "Opportunity, challenge, risk and threat – review of definitions and relations", *Internal Security*, 9(2), 2018, pp. 23–32. https://doi.org/10.5604/01.3001.0012.1699

use historical data and climate forecasts, which can provide valuable information on potential risks. A risk analysis should also include an assessment of the social and economic impacts that may result from flooding in order to be better prepared for possible crises[82].

Based on the risk analysis carried out, the next step is to develop a crisis management strategy. In this phase, it is important to involve various stakeholders, including local authorities (at commune, district and provincial levels), rescue services, and local communities. This collaboration is essential to create a comprehensive plan that takes into account the various aspects of emergency management, such as evacuating residents, securing infrastructure, and communicating with citizens. An effective strategy should be flexible and adaptable to changing conditions, allowing for a faster and more effective response to threats[83].

An important part of preparations for crisis situations is regular drills and exercises to improve the skills of emergency services and local authorities. In the Opolskie Province, the organisation of crisis situation simulations makes it possible to test procedures in practice and identify possible gaps in the system. Such activities are key to building trust among different institutions and increasing the preparedness of local communities for responding to floods[84].

Modern technologies play an important role in the crisis situation planning and preparation process. In the context of flood risk management, the use of early warning systems and tools to monitor hydrological conditions can

---

82 A. Rilo, A. Tavares, P. Freire, P. Santos, J. Zêzere, "The contribution of historical information to flood risk management in the Tagus estuary", *International Journal of Disaster Risk Reduction*, 25, 2017, pp. 22–35. https://doi.org/10.1016/j.ijdrr.2017.07.008; L. Gaňová, M. Zeleňáková, D., Słyś, P. Purcz, "Approach for assessing direct flood damages", *Selected Scientific Papers - Journal of Civil Engineering*, 9(2), 2014, pp. 57–64. https://doi.org/10.2478/sspjce-2014-0016

83 S. Priest, C. Suykens, M. Rijswick, T. Schellenberger, S. Goytia, Z. Kundzewicz, S. Homewood, "The European Union approach to flood risk management and improving societal resilience: lessons from the implementation of the floods directive in six European countries", *Ecology and Society*, 21(4) 2016. https://doi.org/10.5751/es-08913-210450

84 M. Abdel-Mooty, W. El-Dakhakhni, P. Coulibaly, "Data-driven community flood resilience prediction", *Water Policy*, 14(13), 2022, 2120. https://doi.org/10.3390/w14132120; C. Begg, G. Walker, C. Kuhlicke, "Localism and flood risk management in England: the creation of new inequalities?", *Environment and Planning Government and Policy*, 33(4), 2015, pp. 685–702. https://doi.org/10.1068/c12216

significantly increase the effectiveness of rescue efforts. Integrating technology with traditional crisis management methods allows for better forecasting of hazards and faster decision-making in crisis situations[85].

Public education is a key element of emergency preparedness. In the Opolskie Province, local authorities should conduct information campaigns to raise the awareness of residents about flood risks and crisis situation procedures. The communication between emergency services and local communities is of crucial importance, allowing trust to be built, the needs of residents to be better understood, and emergency situations to be handled effectively[86].

Effective flood risk management requires cooperation among different institutions at both the local and regional levels. In the Opolskie Province, it is crucial that emergency services, local authorities, and NGOs work together in joint initiatives and projects. Such cooperation allows for a better use of resources and increases the effectiveness of actions taken in the face of flood risks[87].

Monitoring and evaluation. The final stage in the process of planning and preparing for crisis situations is the monitoring and evaluation of flood risk management measures. Regular evaluation of the effectiveness of implemented policies and procedures allows one to identify areas requiring improvement and to adapt actions to changing conditions. This process is

---

85 L. Solín, M. Madajová, "Spatial planning as a tool of flood risk management in rural landscapes? Position, limitations, and other findings: the case of Myjava region (Slovakia)", *Moravian Geographical Reports*, 31(2), 2023, pp. 106–117. https://doi.org/10.2478/mgr-2023-0010; D. Petrolia, C. Landry, K. Coble, "Risk preferences, risk perceptions, and flood insurance", *Land Economics*, 89 (2), 2013, pp. 227–245. https://doi.org/10.3368/le.89.2.227

86 E. Challies, J. Newig, T. Thaler, E. Kochskämper, M. Levin-Keitel, "Participatory and collaborative governance for sustainable flood risk management: an emerging research agenda", *Environmental Science & Policy*, 55, 2016, 275–280. https://doi.org/10.1016/j.envsci.2015.09.012; L. Solín, M., Madajová, L. Michaleje, "Flood hazards in the headwaters area: lessons learned from a survey of households in the upper Myjava basin, Slovakia", *Water Policy*, 19(6), 2023, 1081–1096. https://doi.org/10.2166/wp.2017.008

87 T. Thi, T. Dinh, M. Helfert, "Modelling collaborative business services", *International Journal of Services Sciences*, 5(1), 2013, 19. https://doi.org/10.1504/ijssci.2013.057649; M. Jailani, "Community-based flood risk management: empowering local responses: a case study in Meru, Klang", *Asian Social Science*, 20(1), 2024, 1. https://doi.org/10.5539/ass.v20n1p1

essential for continuously improving the crisis management system and building the resilience of local communities to flood risks[88].

The crisis situation planning and preparation process in the context of flood risks in the Opolskie Province requires an integrated approach that takes into account both technical and social aspects. Key elements of this process include risk analysis, development of a crisis management strategy, training and drills, use of technology, public education, inter-institutional cooperation, as well as monitoring and evaluation of activities. The cooperation of different stakeholders and the continuous improvement of procedures are essential for effective flood risk management and ensuring the safety of the region's inhabitants.

The role of technology in threat monitoring

In the context of emergency management, particularly in the face of flood risks, technology plays a key role in forecasting and monitoring emergencies. In the Opolskie Province, where the risk of flooding is significant, modern technology is becoming an indispensable tool in effective risk management. Various aspects of the use of technology in threat monitoring and its impact on the effectiveness of rescue operations are discussed below.

One of the most important pieces of technology in threat monitoring is early warning systems. These systems use a variety of data sources, such as meteorological forecasts, hydrological measurements, and satellite data, to predict the occurrence of floods. As Bogdan Ćwik points out, the effectiveness of these systems is based on their ability to process and analyse data quickly, which allows for early detection of warning signals[89]. In the Opolskie Province, such systems are used to monitor water levels in rivers and to forecast the intensity of precipitation, which facilitates adequate preparation for possible risks.

---

88 F. Chan, G. Mitchell, A. McDonald, "Flood risk appraisal and management in megacities: a case study of practice in the Pearl River Delta, China", *Water Practice & Technology*, 7(4), 2012. https://doi.org/10.2166/wpt.2012.060;

89 B. Ćwik, "Threat monitoring in defense and security systems – methodological aspects", *Przegląd Nauk o Obronności*, (5), 2019, pp. 203–229. https://doi.org/10.5604/01.3001.0012.9760

In the context of flood risk monitoring, hydrological technologies play a key role. In the Opolskie Province, modern measuring devices such as water level sensors and rain gauges are used to enable the ongoing monitoring of hydrological conditions. Thanks to the use of IoT (Internet of Things) technology, data from such devices can be transmitted in real time to central crisis management systems, allowing for a quick and ongoing analysis of the situation and initiation of appropriate actions[90].

The use of advanced data analysis algorithms and predictive models is another important aspect of technology in threat monitoring. In the Opolskie Province, analyses of meteorological and hydrological data are performed with the use of numerical models to forecast potential flood scenarios. The use of such models enables a better understanding of the dynamics of hydrological phenomena and the identification of areas most vulnerable to flooding. This helps emergency services to plan preventive actions and respond to crisis situations more effectively.

Technology also plays a major role in crisis communication and information dissemination. In the Opolskie Province, information systems enable information on hazards to be passed on quickly and efficiently to residents and emergency services. The use of social media and mobile applications (during the 2024 flood, this was primarily WhatsApp), allows for up-to-date information on the flood situation and handling procedures to reach the widest possible group of recipients. Effective communication is indispensable in minimising panic and ensuring the safety of residents[91].

The use of technology in threat monitoring also promotes cooperation among the various institutions responsible for crisis management. In the Opolskie Province, emergency services, local authorities, and non-governmental organisations, unfortunately, do not use common information platforms

---

90 D. Savostin-Kosiak, J. Michalski, "Analysis of the impact of road safety barriers on reducing the risk of dangerous road accidents and their consequences", *The National Transport University Bulletin*, 1 (46), 2020, pp. 283–292. https://doi.org/10.33744/2308-6645-2020-1-46-283-292

91 K. Płaciszewski, "E-health – use of information and communications technology (ict) in the Polish health care system", *Medycyna Ogólna i Nauki o Zdrowiu*, 28(2), 2022, pp. 126–131. https://doi.org/10.26444/monz/150276; B. Ćwik, "Threat monitoring in defense and security systems – methodological aspects", *Przegląd Nauk o Obronności*, (5), 2019, pp. 203–229. https://doi.org/10.5604/01.3001.0012.976

to share data and coordinate activities in crisis situations. Cooperation is indispensable for effectively managing flood risk and minimising the impact of disasters[92].

In the context of using technology to monitor potential threats, it is also important to provide training to emergency services and local authorities. In the Opolskie Province, regular training courses are organised on the use of modern monitoring systems and data analysis. Such training improves staff competences and allows for better use of available technology in crisis situations.

The role of technology in monitoring flood risks in the Opolskie Province cannot be overestimated. Early warning systems, hydrological monitoring technologies, data analysis, and effective communication are key elements of effective flood risk management. Cooperation among different institutions and regular training for rescue workers help to increase the efficiency of rescue operations and minimise the consequences of floods. With the increasing risk of floods, further development of technologies and their integration into crisis management systems are becoming essential to ensure the safety of the region's residents.

Coordination of activities in crisis situations

When there is a flood risk, coordination among various emergency rescue services is of primary importance. In the Opolskie Province, in the event of a flood alert, crisis centres and teams (at both the level of local authorities and the level of the services responsible for state security) are set up to coordinate rescue operations and manage resources. Cooperation among the services, as well as with local authorities, is indispensable to ensure the effectiveness of operations and to minimise the consequences of floods.

In crisis situations, such as floods, crisis centres and teams are set up to coordinate rescue efforts. These entities are made up of representatives of various institutions, such as the State Fire Service, the police, the Polish Armed

---

[92] D. Savostin-Kosiak, J. Michalski, "Analysis of the impact of road safety barriers on reducing the risk of dangerous road accidents and their consequences", *The National Transport University Bulletin*, 1(46), 2020, pp. 283–292. https://doi.org/10.33744/2308-6645-2020-1-46-283-292

Forces, local crisis management departments, etc. This cooperation is crucial to ensure cohesion of activities and efficient use of available resources[93]. As Robakowski and Słomiany note, it is important that there is a clearly defined hierarchy and division of roles within crisis centres and teams, which allows for faster decision-making and response to changing conditions[94].

Effective communication among rescue services is essential for the coordination of activities undertaken in crisis situations. In the Opolskie Province, modern communication technologies are used by crisis centres and teams to enable the rapid flow of information. Cooperation with local media and NGOs allows relevant information on hazards and emergency procedures to reach residents. This was perfectly evident in the cooperation between the services and the regional Polish radio station, Radio Opole, which provided the region's inhabitants in real time with up-to-date information on the flood situation, dangers, and evacuation sites. Such messages also helped the services and NGOs to coordinate the management of the humanitarian aid chain. As Filipiak and Dylewski emphasise, it is also crucial that information be communicated in an understandable and accessible manner, which increases the effectiveness of rescue efforts[95].

Cooperation with local communities is a key element of the process of coordinating all activities conducted in crisis situations. In the opinion of the author, local authorities and emergency services in the Opolskie Province do not sufficiently involve residents in the process of planning and preparing for crisis situations. As Morawska, Opach, and Sułkowski, as well as Jończyk and Seliga emphasise, the active involvement of local communities in prevention

---

93 M. Żuber, A. Dziadkiewicz, „Współdziałanie służb, inspekcji i straży na szczeblu powiatu w sytuacjach nadzwyczajnych zagrożeń", *Historia i Polityka*, (23 (30)), 2018, 69. https://doi.org/10.12775/hip.2018.005

94 P. Robakowski, "Crisis safety management in a teaching hospital – a proposal for action (case)", *Journal of Modern Science*, 58(4), 2024, pp. 551–565. https://doi.org/10.13166/jms/192192 and W. Słomiany, „Możliwości wykorzystania systemu logistycznego Sił Zbrojnych Rzeczypospolitej w sytuacjach kryzysowych", *Zeszyty Naukowe Akademii Sztuki Wojennej*, 108(3), 2017, pp. 156–181. https://doi.org/10.5604/01.3001.0010.8421

95 B. Filipiak, M. Dylewski, "Interactions between logistical potential and financial potential in crisis situations - theoretical and methodological approach", *Zeszyty Naukowe Uniwersytetu Szczecińskiego Finanse Rynki Finansowe Ubezpieczenia*, 89, 2017, pp. 343–354. https://doi.org/10.18276/frfu.2017.89/1-28

and education activities increases their resilience to flood risks[96]. This cooperation can take many forms, from organising training events and workshops to setting up local support groups that can act in crisis situations.

Once rescue operations have been completed, it is necessary to carry out an evaluation of the effectiveness of the coordination of activities as well as to identify areas requiring improvement. In the Opolskie Province, after each flood, debriefing meetings are organised with representatives of all institutions involved. As Kowalski and Żuber note, this approach allows lessons to be learnt and procedures to be refined, making rescue operations more effective in the future[97].

Coordination of operations in crisis situations in the Opolskie Province requires an integrated approach that takes into account the cooperation of different institutions, effective communication, regular training, and the involvement of local communities. Such cooperation is essential to minimise the consequences of floods and ensure the safety of the region's residents. It is also crucial to continuously improve procedures and to learn from past experiences in order to be better prepared for future risks.

Cooperation among the police, the State Fire Service, and the Opole Emergency Medical Centre during the flood relief operation in September 2024

Police operations[98]

As early as 13 September 2024, the meteorological services and the Government Security Centre warned of possible intense rainfall, which could lead to flooding in the Dolnośląskie, Opolskie, Śląskie, and Małopolskie Provinces. Due

---

96 K. Kolasińska-Morawska, M. Opach, Ł. Sułkowski, J. Jończyk, R. Seliga, „Zarządzanie sytuacjami kryzysowymi w ratownictwie górskim z wykorzystaniem bezzałogowych statków powietrznych", *International Journal of New Economics and Social Sciences*, 24 (8), 2023, pp. 61–76. https://doi.org/10.5604/01.3001.0054.5463

97 N. Moch, "The potential to respond to crisis situations", *National Security Studies*, 19(1), 2021, pp. 91–112. https://doi.org/10.37055/sbn/146051 and Żuber and Dziadkiewicz, *op. cit.*

98 Information obtained from the Provincial Police Headquarters in Opole on 5.02.2025, document: DK.14684/2025 FINAL REPORT of the commander of the sub-operation "Opole" on the preparation and performance of police actions in connection with the ordered police operation under the code name "FLOOD 2024", prepared by the Chief of Staff of the Commander of the Sub-operation "Opole" – junior inspector Piotr Grudziecki.

to the dynamically deteriorating hydrological situation, a state of natural disaster was declared on 16 September in selected parts of the Dolnośląskie, Opolskie, and Śląskie Provinces. The police implemented Operation FLOOD 2024, under which sub-operation OPOLE was established. On 18 September, an operational plan was drawn up that divided the Opolskie Province into seven operational sections, covering the districts with the greatest exposure to the flood risk: Nysa, Prudnik, Głubczyce, Krapkowice, Brzeg, Opole, and Kędzierzyn-Koźle.

Forces and resources deployed

A total of 13,190 police officers participated in the operation. The average daily number of involved officers was:

- Prevention – 289
- Road traffic – 80
- Criminal division – 154
- Police prevention units and independent police prevention sub-units – 148
- Logistics services – 12

Details are presented in Figure 1.

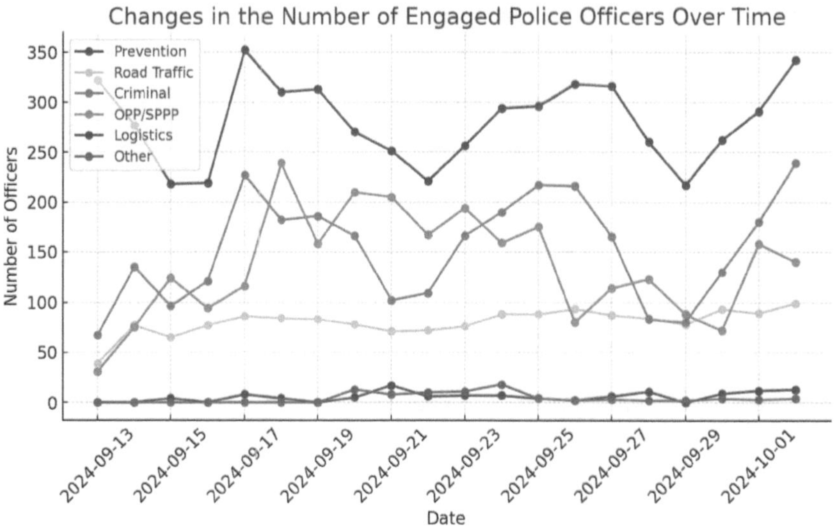

Figure 1: Number of police officers involved in the activities of sub-operation "OPOLE" during the flood in autumn 2024.

Source: the author's own work.

The heaviest workload occurred during the period between 17 and 23 September, when up to 819 police officers per day were on duty. The most police officers were deployed in the districts most affected by the destructive forces of the flood, i.e.: Nyski, Głubczycki, Prudnicki, and Brzeski. The police were assisted in their operations by:

- Military Police – 637 people.
- National Tax Administration – 88 people.
- Road Transport Inspectorate – 39 people.
- Border Guard – 10 people.

The involvement of non-police forces is presented in Figure 2.

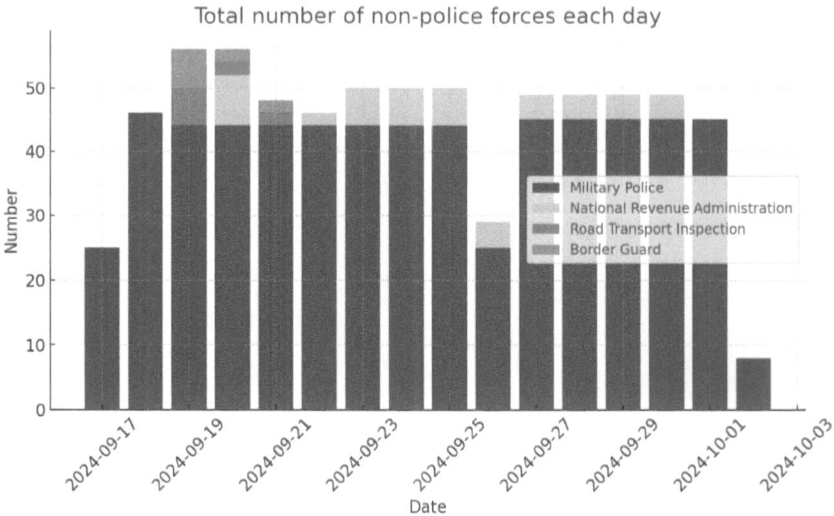

Figure 2: Involvement of non-police forces in sub-operation "OPOLE" during the floods in autumn 2024.

Source: the author's own work based on the data acquired from the Provincial Police Headquarters in Opole.

An average of 250–300 pieces of equipment per day were used by Polish police forces in the Opole region during rescue operations (vehicles, boats, drones, and power generators). The largest volume of equipment

(354 pieces) was used on 17 September. The police provided mobile lighting points, power generators, and dehumidifiers to support the logistics of the operation.

The activities conducted by the police were divided into phases. The first phase involved the evacuation of the population (665 people), especially in the districts of Nysa and Brzeg. Securing road infrastructure – monitoring the passability of roads and bridges and organising diversions. Logistical support – enabling the passage of drinking water tankers and humanitarian convoys. Providing lighting and power to areas without electricity.

The focus of activities in the second phase included securing evacuated areas against theft and vandalism. Humanitarian support – organising shelter for evacuated residents. Provision of technical equipment – dehumidifiers, heaters, and water pumps.

The effects of the flood as estimated by the Provincial Police Headquarters in Opole were as follows:

- Humanitarian losses
  - Evacuation of 665 people:
    - Nyski District – 422 people
    - Brzeski District – 171 people
    - Prudnicki District – 35 people
    - Głubczycki District – 34 people
    - Krapkowice District – 3 people
    - Three fatalities.
- Infrastructural losses
  - Total losses were estimated at PLN 2 billion.
  - Damage to public roads:
    - 4 national roads,
    - 4 provincial roads,
    - 9 district roads.
  - Losses to road infrastructure amounted to PLN 200 million.
- Police losses
  - Four police cars were damaged, resulting in losses of PLN 8,300.
- Crime and related threats

- During the operation, 13 offences and two misdemeanours were recorded, including:
  - Thefts and burglaries in abandoned houses and humanitarian aid warehouses.
  - False offers for the sale of heating equipment (fraudsters impersonating rescue service officers).
  - Looting – 3 people detained.
  - Violence and criminal threats, including against the mayor of Nysa.

Final conclusions

The final report indicates a high level of operational effectiveness but highlights several areas requiring improvement:

1. The effective coordination of activities by the Operations Centre of the Provincial Police Headquarters in Opole allowed rapid responses to a dynamically changing situation.
2. Security of evacuated areas should be improved to reduce incidents of looting and burglary.
3. Better integration between the police and supporting services (e.g. Military Police and Border Guard) should be included in future operational plans.
4. Further monitoring of the effects of the flood and analysis of the existing procedures can improve future rescue operations.

In summary, operation "FLOOD 2024" was well organised and conducted by the Polish Police (including their Opole division), and the rapid responses of the services allowed human and material losses to be minimised. However, additional preventive measures need to be implemented to reduce crime and improve the logistics of rescue operations in the future.

National Fire Service operations[99]

This analysis presents the activities of the State Fire Service (SFS) and the Voluntary Fire Service (VFS) during the flood in the Opolskie Province in

[99] Information obtained from the Spokesperson of the Provincial Commander of the State Fire Service in Opole, Captain Łukasz Nowak, on 20 February 2025.

autumn 2024. The analysis comprises the structure of the deployed forces and resources, the dynamics of the operations, and cooperation with the other rescue services. The data come from an operational report detailing the number of vehicles and rescuers involved.

Rescue activities began on 12 September and continued until mid-October. In the first phase, the deployment of forces was rather moderate, with 28 vehicles and 70 rescuers (SFS and VSF combined) in action on the first day of the operation. The numbers then rose sharply, reaching a peak on 14 September, when 1,109 vehicles and 5,603 people were involved.

The details are shown in Figure 3.

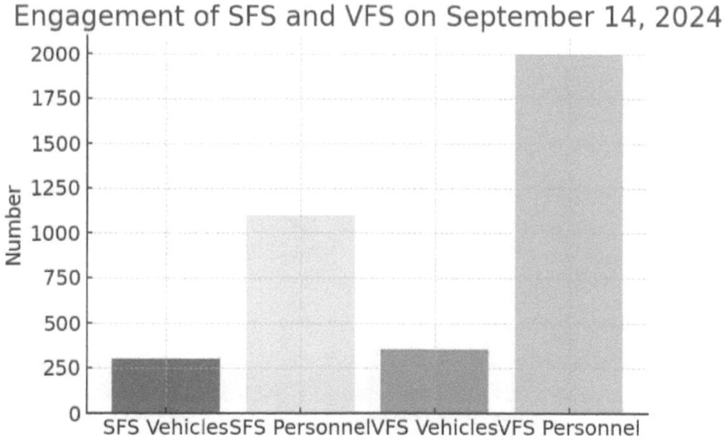

Figure 3: Involvement of SFS and VFS forces on 14 September 2024.
Source: the author's own work based on the data acquired from the Provincial Headquarters of the State Fire Service in Opole.

The largest deployment of forces took place between 13 and 19 September, when the number of rescuers exceeded 4,000 people per day. There was a gradual decline in activity after 19 September as a result of the transition to the flood recovery phase. The operation eventually ended on 15 October, when only 27 vehicles and 60 rescuers participated in final activities.

Division of roles and involvement of individual units

Both local and national SFS and VFS units participated in the rescue operation:

- The central operational reserves of the SFS supplied resources from outside the Opolskie Province, involving a total of 1,139 vehicles and 5,902 rescuers.
- VFS units operating as part of the National Rescue and Firefighting System (NRFS) made the largest contribution to operations, involving 2,310 vehicles and 11,818 volunteers.
- VFS units from outside the NRFS also played a significant role, providing 1,994 vehicles and 10,945 rescuers.

Details are presented in Figure 4.

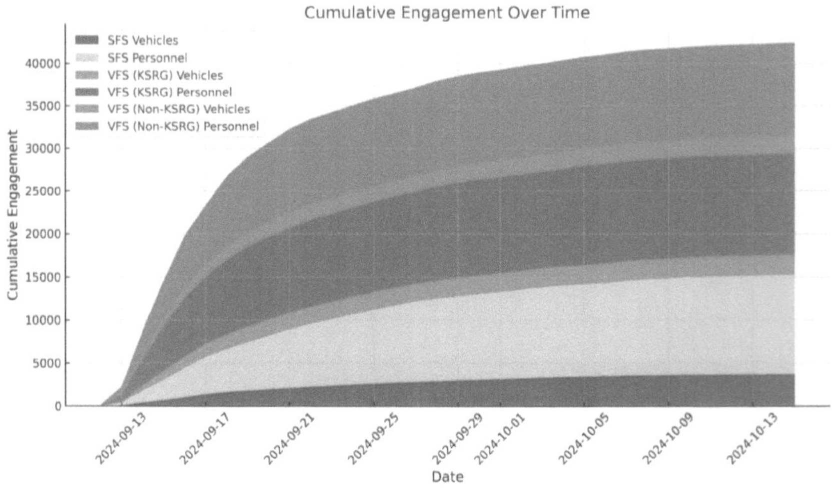

Figure 4: Involvement of the SFS forces and resources in the flood operation in the Opolskie Province.

Source: the author's own work based on the data acquired from the Provincial Headquarters of the State Fire Service in Opole.

The involvement of VFS units shows that volunteers were a key part of the rescue effort, often outnumbering the officers of the SFS. This demonstrates the high mobilisation of local communities in an emergency situation.

A wide range of equipment was used during the operation, including:

- Bagging machines,
- Operational and reconnaissance vehicles,
- Unmanned aircraft,
- Boats and pontoons,
- High-capacity pumps and tankers for transporting drinking water,
- Engineering vehicles (excavators, telescopic loaders).

Additional support was provided by the Polish Armed Forces (including amphibious vehicles, helicopters, engineering equipment), the police (helicopters, quads, and police cars), the Voluntary Water Rescue Service and the Border Guard. A key aspect of the operation's success was the efficient exchange of information among SFS units, as well as cross-border cooperation with the Czech firefighters and other services (Police, Opole Emergency Medical Centre, Polish Armed Forces, etc.).

The rescue operation can be divided into three main stages:

1. Preventive activities – including hazard monitoring, reconnaissance, and floodbank protection.
2. Evacuation and rescue – the most intensive phase of operations, involving the evacuation of the population, the rescue of property, and the maintenance of critical infrastructure.
3. Flood recovery – the phasing out of the operation in which the number of rescuers involved was being gradually reduced.

An analysis of the activities of the SFS and VFS during the flood in the Opolskie Province shows the high efficiency of the emergency rescue system in Poland. The mobilisation of a large number of rescuers in a short space of time, the effective cooperation of the various services, and the use of modern equipment made it possible to limit losses. VFS units played a key role, making up the majority of the rescue forces at the peak of the operation. It is worth noting that effective inter-regional coordination and cooperation with the Czech services significantly improved the effectiveness of the operation.

Activities of the Opole Emergency Medical Centre[100]

This article presents an analysis of the activities of the Emergency Medical Coordination Unit (EMCU) during the flood that affected the Opolskie Province in 2024. The focus was on the process of evacuating medical facilities, the volume of resources involved, and the impact of the conducted activities on the functioning of the emergency medical system in the region.

The analysis is based on operational data on the evacuation of the hospital in Nysa and the care and treatment facility in Paczków. Information on the number of emergency medical teams, air support, and the number of evacuated patients was used. These data allow an assessment of the scale of the intervention and the effectiveness of the measures applied.

Patients were evacuated from two facilities during the flood in the Opolskie Province:

- the hospital in Nysa – 117 patients were evacuated to 15 medical facilities in the region.
- the care and treatment facility in Paczków – 51 patients were evacuated to other care facilities and hospitals.

Details are presented in Table 1.

Table 1: Evacuation of the hospital in Nysa and the care and treatment facility in Paczków by the EMCU medical teams

	Evacuation of the hospital in Nysa and the care and treatment facility in Paczków			
Date	**Medical teams**	**Aircraft**	**P/S**	**Location**
14.09.2024	1	0	S	Paczków
15.09.2024	31	0	P	Nysa
16.09.2024	31	4	P	Nysa
17.09.2024	22	3	P	Paczków
23.09.2024	12	0	P	Paczków
24.09.2024	7	0	P	Paczków

Source: the author's own work.

[100] Information obtained during an individual in-depth personal interview conducted by the author with the Director of the Opole Emergency Medical Centre, Dr. Jarosław Kostyła, on 18 February 2025.

The following were used to carry out the evacuation:

- Emergency Medical Teams: a total of 104 teams were involved on the six key days of the operation (14, 15, 16, 17, 23, and 24 September).
- Air support: a total of 7 helicopters provided by the 25th Air Cavalry Brigade in Tomaszów Mazowiecki were used on 16 and 17 September.
- Personnel: a total of 220 people, including paramedics, physicians, technicians, and administrators, participated in the rescue activities.

The largest mobilisation of resources occurred on 15 and 16 September during the evacuation of the hospital in Nysa, where 31 emergency medical teams were engaged each day and an additional four helicopters on the second day of the operation. The process of relocating the patients of the care and treatment facility in Paczków was spread over several days, allowing for an effective logistical adjustment.

1. Efficiency of operations – the evacuation was carried out without disrupting the activities of the Opolskie Province's Emergency Medical System, indicating the efficiency of the planning and coordination activities of the EMCU.
2. The role of air support – the use of helicopters allowed for faster evacuation at critical times.

The EMCU's activities during the flood proved the high operational efficiency and adaptability of the rescue system. The key success factors included effective coordination ensured by the internal EMCU response team appointed by the EMCU Director, air support, and the mobilisation of additional emergency medical teams. All emergency medical teams used for the evacuation were from outside the Opolskie Province's Emergency Medical System. The EMCU's activities and the medical protection of the inhabitants of the Opolskie Province were not affected in any way by the rescue operations carried out during the flood in autumn 2024.

In the future, it is worth considering further improvements in logistics and communication systems to further reduce emergency response times.

Cooperation is key to successful rescue operations in the Opolskie Province

The flood that hit the Opolskie Province in autumn 2024 was one of the biggest challenges for the local emergency services in more than a decade. Thanks to excellent coordination and close cooperation between the police, the State Fire Service, and the Opole Medical Rescue Centre, with the support of the Polish Armed Forces and other services, it was possible to minimise human losses and limit the consequences of the natural disaster.

The services demonstrated a high level of preparedness and operational efficiency. Preventive measures were taken as early as at the threat forecasting stage, which allowed evacuation plans to be effectively implemented and infrastructure to be secured. The police, in carrying out Operation Flood 2024, not only ensured the safety of residents but also effectively coordinated the logistics of rescue activities. The SFS and VFS, with their vast equipment and human potential, conducted rescue operations in the most difficult conditions, while paramedics from the emergency medical teams ensured the smooth evacuation of medical facilities without disrupting the functioning of the health system.

A key success factor was the effective exchange of information and close cooperation among the services. Joint crisis management centres coordinated the use of resources and cooperation at all administrative levels allowed rapid responses to a dynamically changing situation. This efficient organisation and exemplary cooperation among the various institutions demonstrated that adequate preparation, communication, and joint action constituted the cornerstones of effective crisis management.

The rescue operations during the flood in the Opolskie Province are an example of perfect coordination of the activities of various services, which should be used as a model for future operations of this type. The cooperation among the police, the State Fire Service, and the Emergency Medical Cooperation Unit proved that only by working together can human life and property be effectively protected in the face of natural disasters.

References

ABDEL-MOOTY, M., EL-DAKHAKHNI, W., & COULIBALY, P., "Data-driven community flood resilience prediction", *Water Policy*, 14(13), 2022, 2120. https://doi.org/10.3390/w14132120

BEGG, C., WALKER, G., & KUHLICKE, C., "Localism and flood risk management in England: the creation of new inequalities?", *Environment and Planning C Government and Policy*, 33(4), 2020, 685–702. https://doi.org/10.1068/c12216

CHAN, F., MITCHELL, G., & MCDONALD, A., "Flood risk appraisal and management in mega-cities: a case study of practice in the Pearl River Delta, China", *Water Practice & Technology*, 7(4) 2012. https://doi.org/10.2166/wpt.2012.060

CHALLIES, E., NEWIG, J., THALER, T., KOCHSKÄMPER, E., & LEVIN-KEITEL, M., "Participatory and collaborative governance for sustainable flood risk management: an emerging research agenda", *Environmental Science & Policy*, 55, 2016, pp. 275–280. https://doi.org/10.1016/j.envsci.2015.09.012

ĆWIK, B., "Threat monitoring in defense and security systems – methodological aspects", *Przegląd Nauk O Obronności*, (5), 2019, pp. 203–229. https://doi.org/10.5604/01.3001.0012.9760

DOSTÁL, J. Lessons of cooperation between government and non-governmental organizations in emergency management in the Czech Republic. International Journal of Safety and Security Engineering, 5(3), 2015, pp. 203–221. https://doi.org/10.2495/safe-v5-n3-203-221

FILIPIAK, B., & DYLEWSKI, M., "Interactions between logistical potential and financial potential in crisis situations - theoretical and methodological approach", *Zeszyty Naukowe Uniwersytetu Szczecińskiego Finanse Rynki Finansowe Ubezpieczenia*, 89, 2017, pp. 343–354. https://doi.org/10.18276/frfu.2017.89/1-28

GAŇOVÁ, L., ZELEŇÁKOVÁ, M., SŁYŚ, D., & PURCZ, P., "Approach for assessing direct flood damages", *Selected Scientific Papers - Journal of Civil Engineering*, 9(2), 2014, pp. 57–64. https://doi.org/10.2478/sspjce-2014-0016

HEIJER, F., RIJKE, J., BOSCH-REKVELDT, M., LEEUW, A., & BARCIELA-RIAL, M., "Asset management of flood defences as a co-production—an analysis of cooperation in five situations in the Netherlands", *Journal of Flood Risk Management*, 16(3), 2023. https://doi.org/10.1111/jfr3.12909

JAILANI, M., "Community-based flood risk management: empowering local responses: a case study in Meru, Klang", *Asian Social Science*, 20 (1), 2024, 1. https://doi.org/10.5539/ass.v20n1p1

KLIJN, F., BRUIJN, K., KNOOP, J., & KWADIJK, J., "Assessment of the Netherlands' flood risk management policy under global change", *Ambio*, 41(2), 2011, pp. 180–192. https://doi.org/10.1007/s13280-011-0193-x

KOLASIŃSKA-MORAWSKA, K., OPACH, M., SUŁKOWSKI, Ł., JOŃCZYK, J., & SELIGA, R., „Zarządzanie sytuacjami kryzysowymi w ratownictwie górskim z wykorzystaniem bezzałogowych statków powietrznych", *International Journal of New Economics and Social Sciences*, 24 (8), 2023, pp. 61–76. https://doi.org/10.5604/01.3001.0054.5463

MOCH, N., "The potential to respond to crisis situations", *National Security Studies*, 19(1), 2021, pp. 91–112. https://doi.org/10.37055/sbn/146051

PETROLIA, D., LANDRY, C., & COBLE, K., "Risk preferences, risk perceptions, and flood insurance", *Land Economics*, 89 (2), 2013, pp. 227–245. https://doi.org/10.3368/le.89.2.227

PŁACISZEWSKI, K., "E-health – use of information and communications technology (ICT) in Polish health care system", *Medycyna Ogólna i Nauki o Zdrowiu*, 28(2), 2022, 126–131. https://doi.org/10.26444/monz/150276

PRIEST, S., SUYKENS, C., RIJSWICK, M., SCHELLENBERGER, T., GOYTIA, S., KUNDZEWICZ, Z., & HOMEWOOD, S., "The European Union approach to flood risk management and improving societal resilience: lessons from the implementation of the floods directive in six European countries", *Ecology and Society*, 21(4), 2016. https://doi.org/10.5751/es-08913-210450

RILO, A., TAVARES, A., FREIRE, P., SANTOS, P., & ZÊZERE, J., "The contribution of historical information to flood risk management in the Tagus estuary", *International Journal of Disaster Risk Reduction*, 25, 2017, pp. 22–35. https://doi.org/10.1016/j.ijdrr.2017.07.008

ROBAKOWSKI, P., "Crisis safety management in a teaching hospital – a proposal for action (case)", *Journal of Modern Science*, 58(4), 2024, pp. 551–565. https://doi.org/10.13166/jms/192192

SAVOSTIN-KOSIAK, D., & MICHALSKI, J., "Analysis of the impact of road safety barriers on reducing the risk of dangerous road accidents and their consequences", *The National Transport University Bulletin*, 1(46), 2020, pp. 283–292. https://doi.org/10.33744/2308-6645-2020-1-46-283-292

SOLÍN, Ľ., & MADAJOVÁ, M., "Spatial planning as a tool of flood risk management in rural landscapes? Position, limitations, and other findings: the case of Myjava region (Slovakia)", *Moravian Geographical Reports*, 31(2), 2023, pp. 106–117. https://doi.org/10.2478/mgr-2023-0010

SOLÍN, Ľ., MADAJOVÁ, M., & MICHALEJE, L., "Flood hazards in the headwaters area: lessons learned from a survey of households in the Upper Myjava basin, Slovakia". *Water Policy*, 19(6), 2017, 1081–1096. https://doi.org/10.2166/wp.2017.008

THI, T., DINH, T., & HELFERT, M., "Modelling collaborative business services", *International Journal of Services Sciences*, 5(1), 2013, 19. https://doi.org/10.1504/ijssci.2013.057649

WANG, Q., BAI, Y., & YANG, Y., "The Stackelberg game model of cross-border river flood control", *Frontiers in Ecology and Evolution*, 10, 2022. https://doi.org/10.3389/fevo.2022.964679

WILBY, R., & KEENAN, R., "Adapting to flood risk under climate change", *Progress in Physical Geography Earth and Environment*, 36(3), 2012, pp. 348–378. https://doi.org/10.1177/0309133312438908

WIŚNIEWSKI, B., & KACZMARCZYK, B., "Opportunity, challenge, risk and threat — review of definitions and relations", *Internal Security*, 9(2) 2018, pp. 23–32. https://doi.org/10.5604/01.3001.0012.1699

WIŚNIEWSKI, B., & SANDER, G. S., "Threat, crisis and critical situation – contemporary determinants of modern man's living conditions", *Bezpieczeństwo i Technika Pożarnicza*, (41), 2016, pp. 13–18. https://doi.org/10.12845/bitp.41.1.2016.1

The Role of the Polish Police in Mitigating the Effects of Floods: The Case of the Opolskie and Dolnośląskie Provinces

Rafał Kochańczyk[101]

ABSTRACT
The chapter analyzes the crucial role of the Polish Police in crisis management during floods in the Opole and Lower Silesia voivodeships. The publication highlights the various tasks carried out by the Police, such as public protection, securing infrastructure, evacuation (including air evacuation), escorting, and securing roads, all of which contribute to minimizing the impact of natural disasters. The objective is to emphasize the importance of the Polish Police's involvement in rescue operations and to showcase their role in protecting the lives and property of citizens during floods. By analyzing specific cases and actions taken in the Opole and Lower Silesia voivodeships, the book aims to present best practices and challenges related to coordinating police actions during crises.

Keywords: flood, police, crisis management, Poland

As the main entity responsible for public safety and order, the police, in addition to their basic tasks under the Police Act of 6 April 1990, also perform tasks under the Crisis Management Act. During the 35 years after the transformation of the political system, police officers on numerous occasions and with full dedication took part in many activities related to crisis situations occurring in the territory of Poland and exerted a direct impact on the level of security of people, individual and public property, as well as the natural environment. Over the past 25 years, nearly 100 people died in the three major floods, while the estimated costs associated with property losses amounted to more than PLN 30 billion. This article will outline police operations carried out during the floods that hit southwestern Poland in September 2024.

[101] Superintendent dr Rafał Kochańczyk – Police Officer, on 24 May 2016, he was appointed Commander of the Police Academy in Katowice. In February 2021, he took up the post of Provincial Police Commander in Opole. On 10 January 2024, he was appointed Deputy Police Commander-in-Chief. In the period from 16 September to 30 September 2024, he served as Deputy Commander of the FLOOD 2024 Operation. ORCID: 0000-0002-1432-1927

Introduction

Issues related to safety pertain to both theory and practice. Furthermore, safety as a subject of research is quite complex, partly due to the numerous definitions in the scientific field developed by representatives of various disciplines based on their knowledge, terminology, and the needs of their specific field. Among the many methods used for an in-depth study of a particular safety-related phenomenon, one can distinguish case studies.

The likely pioneers of using this method for research were W. Thomas and R. Parks from the University of Chicago at the beginning of the 20th century[102]. A case study incorporates various other research methods and techniques, including participant observation, document analysis, unstructured interviews, and archival information.

As G. Pare pointed out, case studies can be applied under the following conditions:

- When the phenomenon is broad and complex.
- In situations where existing knowledge is insufficient to pose relevant questions.
- When holistic and in-depth analysis of a phenomenon is required.
- When the phenomenon cannot be studied outside its context[103].

Of course, using this method encounters some challenges, as noted by B. Flyvbjerg[104]:

- It is not possible to make objective generalizations based on one or a few cases.
- This method is mainly suited for pilot studies.
- Another limitation is the significant freedom of interpretation by the researcher, which can make the case study overly subjective.
- Case studies are useful for formulating hypotheses, whereas other methods test hypotheses and build theories.
- This method cannot be used to build theories, as it serves more to gain practical knowledge.

---

[102] J. Hamel, S. Dufour, D. Fortin, *Case study methods*, Sage, Newbury Park, 1993, p. 11.

[103] G. Pare, "Investigating information system with positivist case study research", *Communication Association for Information Systems*, No. 13 (18) 2004, pp. 233–262.

[104] B. Flyvbjerg, „Pięć mitów o badaniach typu studium przypadku", *Studia Socjologiczne*, Nr 2, (177)/2005, pp. 219 – 245.

Nevertheless, despite these objections, the method has been used for many years by representatives of various scientific disciplines both in Poland[105] and worldwide[106]. It allows researchers to confirm, refute, or propose new solutions for existing theories.

The actions taken during the crisis situation of the flood that occurred in September 2024 in the southwestern territory of Poland provided an excellent opportunity to use the case study method because:

- The research process covered various stages of the Polish Police's actions.
- It offered opportunities to observe newly emerging solutions due to the dynamic situation.
- It allowed for direct observation of the actions of various rescue services in areas affected or previously affected by the flood wave.
- It enabled observation of the police's actions in a spatial context.

Flood as a natural phenomenon

The Government Security Centre periodically prepares a risk assessment document for the purposes of crisis management, based on the periodic report on threats to national security and the National Crisis Management Plan[107].

In the National Crisis Management Plan[108], among the 20 descriptions of hazards and risk assessments, flood ranks second, just after epidemic. Events

105 P. Wójcik, *Znaczenie studium przypadku jako metody badawczej w naukach o zarządzaniu*, E-mentor, nr 1(48)/2013, www.e-mentor.edu.pl/artykul/index/numer/48/id/983 [accessed: 20.02.2025 R.]. J.W. Wiktor: *Studium przypadku. Istota, funkcje i procedura analizy przypadku*, (w:) J. Altkorn (red.): *Zarządzanie i przedsiębiorczość. Studia polskich przypadków*, Warszawa-Kraków 1997, p. 11.

106 See more at L. Luck, D. Jackson, K. Usher, "Case study: a bridge across the paradigms", *Nursing Inquiry*, 13(2), 2006, pp. 103–109. https://doi.org/10.1111/j.1440-1800.2006.00309.x [accessed 20.02.2025 r.], W. Tellis, *Introduction to case study. The Qualitative Report*. 1997 https://doi.org/10.46743/2160-3715/1997.2024, [accessed: 20.02.2025 r.], R. K. Yin, *Case Study Research Design and Methods*, Thousand Oaks - London - New Delhi: Sage Publications, 2009.

107 The National Crisis Manegement Plan. https://www.gov.pl/web/rcb/krajowy-plan-zarzadzania-kryzysowego [accessed 26.02.2025].

108 Ibid, Part A, p. 5.

over the centuries show clearly that hazards and the occurrence of floods are a constant element determining various levels of safety. According to Article 16(43) of the Water Act of 20 July 2017[109], a flood is defined as "a temporary covering by water of land that is not normally covered by water, in particular caused by freshets of water in natural watercourses, reservoirs, canals, and from the sea, excluding a covering by water of land caused by surges of water in sewerage systems".

The risk of flooding varies and depends on a number of factors such as, for example, population density, the use of river valleys and floodplains, technical and communication infrastructure, and, particularly in recent years, the changing climate.

We distinguish the following types of floods:

I. With regard to scope:
   - a local flood - a flooding usually caused by heavy torrential rainfall, covering small drainage basins,
   - a regional flood - a flood affecting a water region, often caused by frontal rainfall,
   - a nationwide flood - a flood that covers a significant area of a river basin, the main cause of which is prolonged rainfall over large areas, extensive rainfall.

II. With regard to source:
   - a fluvial flood - a flood associated with the overflow of water in rivers, streams, canals, mountain torrents, and lakes, including a flood resulting from melting snow,
   - a precipitation flood - a flood associated with the inundation of land with water coming directly from rainfall or snow melt; it may include urban storm floods or excess water in non-urban areas,
   - a groundwater flood - a flood associated with the inundation of land due to water levels rising above ground level; it may include groundwater rises resulting from high surface water levels,
   - a seaward flood - a flood associated with the inundation of land by seawater, including estuarine sections of rivers and coastal lakes,

[109] Ct. Journal of Laws of 2024, item 1087.

- a flood from hydrotechnical facilities - a flood associated with the inundation of land by water caused by a failure of damming structures,
- other floods - floods caused by other factors and floods of unknown origins.

III. With regard to mechanism:
- a natural surge - the inundation of land due to a rise in water levels,
- an overflow of water over flood defences - the inundation of land as a result of water overflowing, for example, over the crown of a flood barrier,
- a failure of flood defences or technical infrastructure - the inundation of land as a result of a destruction or failure of natural or artificial flood defences or technical infrastructure, including a failure of retention facilities, flood gates,
- embacle flood - the inundation of land due to the formation of a natural or artificial blockage on a watercourse,
- backwater - the backing up of water caused by the occurrence of strong winds from the sea, the occurrence of an ice or slush blockage, or the operation of a hydrotechnical facility at sea, in bays and basins, causing water to be forced upstream,
- a flash flood - a special case of a precipitation (torrential) flood of a local scope, very rapid course and short duration (usually less than 6 hours), caused by rainfall with a high yield, often of a thunderstorm nature; it can happen anywhere, most often in mountainous areas; favourable conditions for its occurrence are also in urban areas (urban flood),
- other - the inundation of land by water due to another or unknown mechanism.[110]

Police in the crisis management system

The variety of the aforementioned hazards indicates that a systemic approach, understood as a holistic and orderly system, a set of objects, principles and assertions, rules of conduct, is necessary when carrying out crisis management tasks. Only such an approach can ensure the effective and efficient

110 The National Crisis Management Plan ..., op. cit.

action of multiple actors with different competences, forces, and resources. An important element of this system is the police, who, in addition to their basic tasks such as ensuring public safety and order and hunting offenders and criminals, also perform crisis management tasks.

This thesis is confirmed by Article 14 of the Crisis Management Act, which indicates that the provincial governor, as the competent authority for crisis management in the province, fulfils their tasks in cooperation with, among other entities, the police. These tasks may include the following:

- directing, monitoring, planning, responding to, and eliminating consequences of hazards in the territory of the province;
- implementing civil planning tasks, including:
  - making recommendations for district heads with regard to district crisis management plans;
  - approving district crisis management plans;
  - preparing and submitting the provincial crisis management plan for approval to the minister responsible for public administration;
  - implementing guidelines for provincial crisis management plans;
  - managing, organising and conducting crisis management training, exercises, and workshops;
  - performing activities resulting from planning documents drawn up as part of provincial operational planning activities;
  - preventing, countering and dealing with the consequences of terrorist incidents;
  - organising the performance of critical infrastructure protection tasks.

In addition to the tasks outlined in the Crisis Management Act, the police have developed their own crisis situation response procedures for the following types of natural calamities:[111]

- natural disasters: floods, fires, and intense precipitation (rain, snow, hail);

[111] Prepared on the basis of Regulation no. 1429 of the Police Commander-in-Chief of 31 December 2004, on the implementation of emergency response procedures in the police services, Journal of the Regulations of the Police Commander-in-Chief, no. 3, item 8.

- technical failures, i.e. construction disasters, releases of hazardous chemicals in (road, rail, pipeline, sea, and inland waterway) transport, industry, and storage, as well as failures of power generation and distribution systems;
- infectious diseases of humans, animals, and plants.

Considering the crisis situations listed above, it can be concluded that the police are one of the main actors involved in all phases of crisis management, i.e. prevention, preparation, response, and recovery. The specific tasks of the police forces in the individual phases of crisis management can be presented as follows[112]:

· Prevention phase

Tasks in this phase include activities aimed at eliminating or reducing the likelihood of a hazard occurring or efforts to reduce its impact. Such activities consist of the following:

- conducting an ongoing analysis of situations that may give rise to hazards;
- participating in the development of legislation by the competent authorities to limit the possibility of a hazard occurring;
- enforcing compliance with the regulations issued by the competent authorities.

· Preparation phase

In this phase, planning activities are carried out using information from other actors together with determining how to respond to a hazard (organisation of the command post and communication systems, development of alert systems). Furthermore, forces and resources are gathered by collecting relevant data on resources, appropriate equipment for officers; training, exercises, and drills necessary for a proper response are organised and conducted.

112 Prepared on the basis of Regulation no. 24 of the Police Commander-in-Chief of 10 November 1998, on the performance of tasks by the police in conditions of natural disasters and technical failures, Journal of the Regulations of the Police Commander-in-Chief, 1998, no. 7.

- Response phase

It is possible to distinguish two stages in the activities of the police in this phase. The first is the initial stage of receiving information about an incident, carrying out verification, notifying other services and actors, and sending forces and resources to the site of an incident. The second stage in this phase includes activities such as alerting, warning, ensuring the circulation of information, as well as taking steps to ensure the protection of public safety and order, the proper securing of communication routes, direct rescue operations, and processual incident documentation.

- Recovery phase

In the last element of crisis management, the police's activities are oriented towards ensuring safety and public order in the area where rescue operations have been carried out, including securing access routes for both emergency services and evacuees, performing processual activities in connection with an incident. An important element in this phase is analysing the activities of individual units and, on this basis, formulating conclusions, making adjustments to plans, and, on the basis of experience, introducing new solutions to the operations of the police forces.

Case study

On 11 September 2024, a briefing was organised at the Government Security Centre during which an order was issued to monitor the hydrometeorological situation in the country. To this end, an order was issued via the GSC duty service to the provincial commanders in Łódź, Opole, Poznań, and Wrocław to immediately establish contact with the provincial crisis management centres and to maintain prevention division officers' full readiness for action, in particular with regard to road traffic organisation and management.

The above instructions were intended to support activities aimed at preventing and responding to flooding and waterlogging events.

In such circumstances, the main tasks for the police include the following:

- in the road traffic area – closing or clearing roads and traffic routes,
- assistance to rescue entities (including mainly state fire brigades, volunteer fire brigades, and state medical emergency services).

Taking into account the flood situation, in accordance with Regulation no. 36 of the Police Commander-in-Chief[113], procedures were implemented regarding the following factors:

- hazards to human life and health and to the environment resulting from the occurrence of a flood;
- significant property losses, damage to residential, business, and public buildings and facilities;
- the occurrence of breaches of public order, including in areas where evacuees are housed and where humanitarian aid is distributed;
- damage to road, rail, air, or water transport infrastructure resulting in restrictions, disorganisation, or complete paralysis of transport;
- failure of the population to comply with instructions and orders issued by the rescue and law enforcement services;
- devastation or theft of private and public property left behind during the evacuation of the population from a factually or potentially dangerous area;
- panic at the site of ongoing rescue operations as well as disruption of public safety and order;
- obstruction of road, rail, air, or water transportation routes caused by massive uncontrolled movement of people to areas not affected by floods.

Chronology of activities

On 11 September 2024, at a briefing held at the Government Security Centre with the participation of the First Deputy Commander-in-Chief, among other things, a decision was taken to monitor the hydrometeorological situation in the territory of the whole country. As a result of the above (via the duty service of the Police Headquarters), the Provincial Police Commanders in Łódź, Opole, Poznań, and Wrocław received instructions:

- to establish immediate contact with the Provincial Crisis Management Centres,

---

[113] Regulation no. 36 of the Police Commander-in-Chief of 14 November 2017 on *tasks to be performed by the police during crisis situations and other incidents*, Journal of the Regulations of the Commander-in-Chief of the Police, 2017, no. 13, as amended.

- to maintain prevention division officers' full readiness for action, in particular with regard to road traffic organisation and management.

The above instructions were intended to support activities focused on preventing and responding to flooding and waterlogging events. In such situations, the main tasks of the police include the following: closing or clearing roads and traffic routes and supporting the efforts of the Provincial Crisis Management Centres, the Volunteer Fire Brigade, and the State Fire Service to minimize the potential consequences of crisis events caused by heavy rainfall. On 12 September 2024, the First Deputy Police Commander gave the designated police organisational units written instructions:

1) to proceed with the performance of tasks, in particular with regard to:
   - ensuring public safety and order in the area of operations, including the outlining of detours,
   - establishing cooperation and information exchange with public administration bodies (e.g. provincial governors, provincial inspectors of environmental protection, representatives of the regional water management authorities) and other institutions competent for dealing with the effects of floods,
   - obtaining information on the location and scale of incidents,
   - providing assistance in the event that the evacuation of persons and property is ordered,
   - securing the property of the evacuated population at their storage points,
   - carrying out procedural tasks related to incidents (e.g. determining the victims or casualties),
   - informing the media of dangers and impediments to movement.

On 16 September 2024, the First Deputy Police Commander issued written instructions on:

1) updating the alert lists in the subordinate police prevention units and the independent police prevention sub-units, taking into account the possible deployment of 30 compact sub-units to support operations in the territory of the country;
2) maintaining continuity of service within the Police Commander-in-Chief's central reserves in accordance with the schedule for September 2024.

On 13 September 2024, at 8.00 a.m. (until further notice), the Police Commander-in-Chief's Operations Centre and the Operations Centres of the Provincial Police Headquarters, functioning on a 24/7 basis, were established in Opole, Wrocław, Katowice, Rzeszów, Poznań, Bydgoszcz, Łódź, Kielce, and Gorzów Wlkp. for the purpose of the ongoing monitoring of the course of events and systematically analysing the information obtained and updating the data on police forces and resources used in operations. On the basis of Regulation no. 20 of the Police Commander-in-Chief of 13 July 2020 on the methods and forms of preparation and implementation of police actions in connection with special events, the units mentioned below were ordered to prepare and carry out activities in the form of a police operation:

- **Provincial Police Headquarters in Opole**
  13.09.2024 – 16.09.2024 a police operation called "WATER 2024". Chief of the operation – Provincial Police Commander in Opole.
- **Provincial Police Headquarters in Wrocław**
  13.09.2024 – 16.09.2024 a police operation called "Flood". Chief of the operation - First Deputy Provincial Police Commander in Wrocław.

On 14 September 2024, additional forces and support resources were deployed from individual police units in the areas subordinate to the Provincial Police Commanders in Wrocław and Opole to carry out tasks consisting of the following:

- providing assistance in the evacuation of persons and property, also with the assistance of police aviation resources,
- organising bypasses in the areas at risk of flooding and providing information on such bypasses,
- securing property left behind by evacuees.

On 15 September 2024, the Air Operations Coordination Centre "FLOOD 2024" was launched at the Main Staff of the Chief Police Headquarters for the purpose of rapid exchange of information between the representatives of the police and border guard airborne units and the Polish Armed Forces and the State Fire Service.

On 16 September 2024, the provincial police headquarters received the Regulation of the Council of Ministers of 16 September 2024 on the introduction of a state of natural disaster in parts of the Dolnośląskie, Opolskie, and Śląskie provinces and were instructed to make sure that police officers assigned to operations in the districts covered by the state of natural disaster become familiar with and comply with the content of the regulation.

On 16 September 2024, at 9.00 p.m., a decision of the Police Commander-in-Chief ordered the police operation "FLOOD 2024", including the appointment of a staff of the police operation chief, for the purpose of ensuring the proper organisation and coordination of activities related to the preparation and management of the operation. The 1st Deputy Police Commander-in-Chief was appointed as the head of the operation. *A Plan of Action for the chief of the police operation code-named "FLOOD 2024"* was developed and delivered to the police organisational units involved in the operation.

On 17 September 2024, the Logistics Office of the Police Headquarters approached the Government Strategic Reserves Agency with a request to provide the police forces with additional resources, which resulted in the deployment of the following equipment:

Specification	Number	Comments
TYCHEM overalls	1000 pcs.	decision of the Minister of the Interior and Administration no. 49/R/24 of 19.09.2024
Nitrile gloves	10000 pcs.	
Stainless steel cup	500 pcs.	
Rubber boots	500 pairs	
Mobile lighting – searchlight	15 sets	decision of the Minister of the Interior and Administration no. 50/R/24 of 19.09.2024
Camo 2 headlamp	100 sets	
Torch with signal cap	100 sets	
Sandbag	5000 pcs.	
Submersible pump 250 m3/h	2 pcs.	decision of the Minister of the Interior and Administration no. 51/R/24 of 19.09.2024
Lighting mast	5 pcs.	
Lighting mast	19 pcs.	decision of the Minister of the Interior and Administration no. 84/R/24 of 03.10.2024
Generator set up to 50 kW	1 pc.	
Heater 230V	25 pcs.	

Source: author's own work based on data from the Police Headquarters.

On 21 September 2024, the Operations Commander ordered the termination of activities in the sub-operations "KRAKÓW" and "RZESZÓW".

On 8 September 2024 at 2.00 p.m., the Operations Commander ordered the termination of activities in the sub-operations "KATOWICE" and "POZNAŃ".

On 30 September 2024, the Operations Commander announced that the Air Operations Coordination Centre was closing at 9.00 p.m. At 2.00 p.m. the Operations Commander ordered the termination of activities in the police operation "FLOOD 2024".

Activities of the air operations coordination centre

An important element during the operations described was the use of aircraft. Between 15 and 30 September 2024, the Air Operations Coordination Centre FLOOD 2024 was functioning at the Main Staff of the Chief Police Headquarters for the purpose of rapid exchange of information between the representatives of the police and Border Guard airborne units, and the Polish Armed Forces and the State Fire Service, which allowed helicopters to be quickly sent to the most threatened areas, as required.

The centre had a total of 25 aircraft at its disposal, i.e.: the police – 6 aircraft, the Polish Armed Forces – 14 aircraft, the Border Guard – 3 aircraft and the Czech Air Force – 2 aircraft.

A total of 303 flights were made, including:

- 217 patrol flights (Police – 106, Polish Armed Forces and Czech Air Force – 86, Border Guard – 25);
- 34 evacuation flights (Police – 13, Polish Armed Forces and Czech Air Force – 19, Border Guard – 2);
- 52 transport flights (Police – 14, Polish Armed Forces and Czech Air Force – 31, Border Guard – 7);
- within the scope of the transport flights, the helicopters moved a total of 784 Big Bags.

Persons evacuated by aircraft

It is important to bear in mind that evacuating people by air from endangered areas due to difficult weather conditions (rain, wind) is a very complex operation during which the life and health of both evacuees and rescuers are at risk. For the most part, this type of action could have been avoided if people had complied with official instructions and had left their homes by land on their own while it was still possible.

During the operations conducted between 13 September and 2 October, 199 people were evacuated by means of aircraft (Police – 99, Polish Armed Forces and Czech Air Force – 98, Border Guard – 2).

Number of deaths

From 14 September 2024 until the end of the operation, nine corpses were detected:

1. The Provincial Police Headquarters in Katowice (the District Police Headquarters in Bielsko- Biała): on 14 September 2024, in the city of Bielsko-Biała at ul. Pileckiego, under the bridge, in the bed of the stream flowing down from the mountains – Kamienie no. 1, the body of a man aged 42 was found.
2. The Provincial Police Headquarters in Opole (the District Police Headquarters in Nysa): on 16 September 2024 at 00.15 a.m., in the city of Nysa at ul. Jagiellońska, firefighters found in the water the corpse of Krzysztof K., aged 71, reported missing on 15 September 2024 at 7.20 p.m. at the City Police Headquarters in Nysa.
3. The Provincial Police Headquarters in Opole (the District Police Headquarters in Nysa): on 17 September 2024, at 2.37 p.m., in the village of Nowy Świętów, in the Biała Głuchołaska river, a body of a woman aged approximately 50–60 years was found.
4. The Provincial Police Headquarters in Opole (the District Police Headquarters in Nysa): on 26 September 2024, in the course of activities connected with the flood operation, a soldier of the Polish Armed Forces, in a field in the commune of Bodzanów-Rudawa discovered the body of a woman aged approximately 50–60 years. Preliminary findings indicated that it may have been a woman reported missing in the Czech Republic.
5. The Provincial Police Headquarters in Wrocław (the District Police Headquarters in Kłodzko): on the night of 14/15 September 2024, in the village of Krosnowice, in a flooded single-family house, the body of a man aged 58 was found submerged in the water.
6. The Provincial Police Headquarters in Wrocław (the District Police Headquarters in Kłodzko / the police station in Lądek Zdrój): on

15 September 2024, in the town of Lądek-Zdrój, police officers discovered the body of a woman in her 70s during a rescue operation in one of the flats. The Provincial Police Headquarters in Wrocław (the District Police Headquarters in Kłodzko / the police station in Lądek Zdrój): on 17 September 2024, at about 11.30 a.m., in the town of Lądek Zdrój, police officers received information about a Dacia passenger car with a man's body inside.

7. The Provincial Police Headquarters in Wrocław (the District Police Headquarters in Kłodzko / the police station in Stronie Śląskie): on 17 September 2024, in the town of Stronie Śląskie, officers of the police station in Lądek Zdrój, while performing their duties, discovered the corpse of Andrzej L., aged 67 years, in the riverbed of the Biała Lądecka river.
8. The Provincial Police Headquarters in Wrocław (the District Police Headquarters in Kłodzko): on 26 September 2024, soldiers of the Polish Armed Forces, performing cleaning works in the area of an agricultural farm in the village of Ołdrzychowice Kłodzkie, discovered the body of a 76-year-old woman, for whom a search had been conducted since 19 September 2024.

Forces and resources deployed

From the beginning of operations, police officers were deployed a total of 53,370 times to carry out flood-related tasks on a multiple basis, including:

- prevention – 22,590;
- road traffic – 8,084;
- criminal division – 9,463;
- prevention units – 12,899;
- logistics – 189;
- others – 145.

During the FLOOD 2024 operation, a total of 21,438 vehicles at the disposal of the police were used, including:

- motor vehicles – 20,999;
- coaches – 7;
- boats – 285;
- jet skis – 24;
- unmanned aircraft – 61.

Ensuring communication systems in flood-affected areas

It should be recognized that in addition to ensuring the physical safety of individuals affected by the flood, providing a communication system played a significant role for both the services carrying out tasks in these areas and the local community. As a result of the destructive force of the water, both traditional and mobile communication networks were destroyed. The only system available to the services, state, and local authorities was the radio communication system.

Ensuring communication during this operation required mobilizing adequate personnel and equipment resources, as well as organizing close cooperation between various police units and external entities. Tasks related to organizing and ensuring safety during the operation also demanded rapid response, system reliability, and proper organization of communication, coordination, and command.

Actions undertaken included activating video services in the command center of the Dolnośląskie Voivodeship Office, equipping the meeting hall with sound systems, ensuring LTE connectivity for videoconferencing needs, and configuring connections for the Police Videoconferencing System.

Examples of Telecommunication Infrastructure Development in Dolnośląskie Voivodeship:

- Deployment of a mobile TETRA base station at the District Police Headquarters in Kłodzko.
- Deployment of another mobile TETRA base station using a mobile command unit from the Central Anti-Terrorist Unit (BOA) at a military site in Kłodzko.
- Installation of an SDWAN network node at the police station in Polanica-Zdrój, enabling multiple Internet access methods using satellite technology.
- Establishment of radio and telephone communications at the police station in Lądek-Zdrój using the TETRA Police Radiocommunication System through a mobile TETRA base station for Lądek-Zdrój, Stronie Śląskie, and surrounding areas.
- Installation of an SRP-T base station and teleinformatics node for Poland's National Teleinformatics Network's emergency number (112) at a new site in Kamieniec Police Station, ensuring connectivity via satellite and redundant cellular networks.

- Provision of six satellite communication kits for data transmission.
- Testing and activation of video transmission from a Bell 407 police helicopter.

It's worth highlighting that police specialists ensured the TETRA signal in Kłodzko County for the police, Ministry of National Defense (including the Military Hospital in Lądek-Zdrój), Armed Forces, and other non-police users with compatible devices.

Selected actions in Opole Voivodeship

- Establishment of a backup command post for the District Police Headquarters in Nysa.
- Installation of a satellite data transmission kit on a vehicle used by the Non-Standard Team for Missing Persons Search in Open Areas, from the Independent Prevention Unit in Opole.
- Delivery of IT equipment necessary for staff operations, analysis, and event recording in post-flood areas.

Other efforts during flood response operations

- Providing videoconferencing services for the Prime Minister using the police videoconferencing network.
- Streaming live video via the police videoconferencing network from a police helicopter and five unmanned aerial vehicles operated by the State Fire Service.
- Ensuring access to video streams from unmanned aerial vehicles of the State Fire Service and the Ministry of National Defense.
- Procurement of 70 satellite communication kits (Starlink) from the Government Agency for Strategic Reserves.
- Securing 100 radios from the Communication and IT Bureau of the Police Headquarters for field units operating in flood-affected areas.

SWOT analysis of police operations during the September 2024 flood

Since the author participated in the FLOOD 2024 operations in Opole and Dolnośląskie Voivodeships, a SWOT analysis was prepared based on knowledge of crisis management, available reports, daily briefings, and direct observations. This heuristic technique is widely popular and frequently applied in management sciences to organize and analyze information. When conducting this analysis, strong and weak points of the institution are identified, alongside opportunities and threats. This helps establish areas for improvement, growth opportunities, and challenges to mitigate. This method serves as a summary of operations and presents conclusions drawn from crisis response actions.

Table 1: SWOT analysis of police activities during the flood in September 2024

Strengths	**Weaknesses**
Police units are located in every county.	Persistent level of vacancies in local police units.
Funded by the state budget.	Lack of specialized equipment in areas prone to flooding.
Police have well-prepared and experienced crisis management personnel.	Limited regional crisis management training for local authorities and rescue entities.
Capability to quickly deploy resources from other regions during floods.	Lack of professional training for irregular incidents.
Possess various equipment usable during flood operations.	Police infrastructure (mainly buildings) is not suited for prolonged operations in case of flooding.
Opportunities	**Threats**
Equipping units participating in flood operations with better resources.	Insufficient funding for crisis situations.
Raising awareness among officers through training and exercises on crisis actions.	Crisis situations managed by inexperienced officers.
Implementation of modern technologies to support crisis operations.	Overlapping responsibilities during flood crises, including aiding other services.
The presence of local officers in communities contributes significantly to safety.	Crisis situations might lead to exploitation of affected residents, such as illegal fundraising.
Possibility of educating local communities about proper crisis responses.	Lack of legal regulations complicates efforts to reduce misinformation in flood-prone areas.

Source: own study.

Based on the conducted SWOT analysis, it can be concluded that the police are a crucial entity within the crisis management system, both in its formal and functional dimensions. An advantage of this formation is the distribution of police units, covering both counties and individual municipalities. Obtaining secured financing from the state budget significantly influences the efficiency of operations. The threats that need to be eliminated primarily concern formal aspects, such as current legal regulations and the insufficient training system in crisis management.

Conclusions

The legal regulations in force in Poland with regard to crisis management set out tasks at all levels of central government and local government administration units. The National Crisis Management Plan quite precisely describes natural hazards that may occur in the territory of Poland. Although in the basic tasks of the police there is no reference to actions during natural disasters, in the case of such circumstances, thanks to internal regulations, the police have appropriate procedures to be employed in all four phases of crisis management. The main task of police officers during operations relating to natural disasters, including floods, is the typical service associated with broadly defined policing. In addition, it is possible to distinguish three more segments of police activity, namely rescue operations, collaboration with other rescue services, and investigation. A very important element in these types of activities is to provide information on existing risks and hazards to as many people as possible who could be affected by floods. In this type of hazard, it is very important that the various services and institutions work together. The actions of the Polish police during the FLOOD 2024 operation demonstrated their professionalism and commitment in all tasks carried out, with the use of a range of equipment from drones to heavy Black Hawk helicopters.

References

Regulation no. 1429 of the Police Commander-in-Chief of 31 December 2004 on the implementation of emergency response procedures in the police, Journal of the Regulation of the Police Commander-in-Chief,

2005, no. 3, item 8. https://www.gov.pl/web/rcb/krajowy-plan-zarzadzania-kryzysowego

HAMEL J., DUFOUR S., FORTIN D., *Case Study Methods*, Sage, Newbury Park, 1993.

PARE G., "Investigating information systems with positivist case study research", *Communication Association for Information Systems*, No. 13 (18) 2004, pp. 233–262.

FLYVBJERG B., "Five Myths About Case Study Research", *Studia Socjologiczne*, No. 2, (177), 2005, pp. 219–245.

WÓJCIK P., *The Importance of Case Study as a Research Method in Management Sciences, E-mentor,* No. 1(48)/2013, available at www.e-mentor.edu.pl/artykul/index/numer/48/id/983 [accessed 20.02.2025].

WIKTOR J. W., *Case Study: Essence, Functions, and Procedure of Case Analysis*, (in:) J. Altkorn (ed.): *Management and Entrepreneurship: Studies of Polish Cases*, Warsaw-Cracow 1997.

LUCK, L., JACKSON, D., & USHER, K., *Case Study: A Bridge Across the Paradigms*, *Nursing Inquiry*, 13(2), 2006, pp. 103–109. https://doi.org/10.1111/j.1440-1800.2006.00309.x [accessed 20.02.2025].

TELLIS, W., *Introduction to Case Study*, *The Qualitative Report*, 1997. https://doi.org/10.46743/2160-3715/1997.2024 [accessed 20.02.2025].

YIN R. K.: *Case Study Research Design and Methods*, 5th Edition. Thousand Oaks - London - New Delhi: Sage Publications, 2009.

Regulation no. 20 of the Police Commander-in-Chief of 13 July 2020 on the methods and forms of preparation and performance of police activities in connection with special events, 2020, item 35.

The Police Act of 6 April 1990, c.t. Journal of Laws of 2024, item 145, as amended.

The Crisis Management Act of 26 April 2007, c.t. Journal of Laws of 2024, item 834.

The Water Act of 20 July 2017, Journal of Laws 2024, item 1087.

The Regulation of the Council of Ministers of 16 September 2024 on the introduction of a state of natural disaster in the territory of parts of the Dolnośląskie, Opolskie and Śląskie provinces, Journal of Laws of 2024, item 1365.

Regulation no. 24 of the Police Commander-in-Chief of 10 November 1998 on the performance of tasks by the police in conditions of natural disasters and technical failures, Journal of the Regulations of the Police Commander-in-Chief, 1998, no. 7.

Regulation no. 36 of the Police Commander-in-Chief of 14 November 2017 on tasks performed by the Police in crisis situations and other incidents, Journal of the Regulations of the Police Commander-in-Chief, 2017, no. 13, as amended.

The case of the contamination of the Odra River. What went wrong?

Anita Dmitruczuk[114]

ABSTRACT

The response of state institutions to the environmental crisis that occurred on the Odra River in the summer of 2022 is far from satisfactory. The dead fish were being removed from the river for several days by anglers and volunteers, and the ineffective efforts in this regard led to a secondary contamination of the river. Although reports of mass fish deaths had been appearing since the end of July, for ten days they were treated as local events. The failure to identify river pollution as a threat included in the National Emergency Management Plan contributed to the failure to give them their due prominence. The disastrous circulation of information and the dispersion of responsibility regarding the management of water resources contributed to ineffective management. Public institutions also appear to have underestimated a new type of non-military threat combining both the complexity of processes and the uncertainty of the effects of actions taken.

Keywords: contamination, flood, crisis management, river, Poland

Introduction. The environmental crisis on the Odra River

The Odra River is the third longest river in Poland. It takes its source in the Czech Republic, and at the same time it forms the border between Poland and Germany over a length of 161 km, previously flowing through heavily industrialised Upper and Lower Silesia. Both the transboundary nature of the Odra, its size and the fact that it is an artery connecting areas of coal and copper mining as well as a number of manufacturing plants influenced the interest in the contamination of the river in the summer of 2022. Another important factor was the magnitude of the disaster, which the European Commission and the European Environment Agency[115] described as one of the biggest environmental disasters in the modern history of European rivers. The management of this crisis was marked by uncertainty about the causes

---

[114] Anita Dmitruczuk, Research Assistant, University of Opole, Department of Governance and Public Policy.

[115] Free et al. (2023)

of the disaster until 19 August, when the Polish Minister of the Environment presented a hypothesis at an inter-ministerial crisis team meeting suggesting that the river had been contaminated by the toxic algal bloom identified as *Prymnesium parvum*[116]. Prior to this date, the actions of the public authorities were carried out under conditions of ignorance and the emergence of competing hypotheses on the causes of the contamination, which should be taken into account when assessing the effectiveness of public policies and the efficiency of emergency management related to the environmental disaster.

It is not clear when the disaster started or how many aquatic organisms died in connection with it. According to a report by the Supreme Audit Office (NIK), 250 tons of dead fish were caught along a several-hundred-kilometre section of the Polish river, while German authorities reported another 100 tons.[117] The figure of 360 tons including mussels is provided by a European Commission[118] analysis based on Polish and German sources. On the other hand, in the scientific literature, the mortality of living organisms during the ecological catastrophe was estimated at as much as 1650 tons, which would mean a reduction in the fish population by 60 per cent.[119] The uncertainty about the magnitude of the environmental consequences of the contamination of the Odra River is due, among other things, to the late response of the state and the simultaneous lack of testing along the entire length of the river. In the first phase of the crisis, volunteers and the Polish Angling Association were responsible for extracting fish from the river, the biomass was not weighed and some of the dead fish fell to the bottom, decomposing and thus exacerbating the environmental crisis.

The presence of dead fish in the Gliwicki Canal was first reported as early as March 2022. After routine investigations, the cause of their death was not established. Further information appeared in mid-July in the Opole section of the Kędzierzyński Canal. At that time, hypoxia was ruled out as the cause, and this information was communicated as part of the International Warning and Alert Plan for the Odra River. No such action was taken on

---

116 NIK (2023), p. 31.
117 NIK, 2023, p. 7
118 Free et al., 2023
119 Szlauer-Łukaszewska et al., 2024

27 July, when dead fish appeared in the Odra River at Oława. Water tests at the time showed elevated oxygen levels, but this information was not passed on.

- On 1 August, information about dead fish and possible pollution resulting in an ecological disaster was communicated by the Mayor of Oława to the Provincial Crisis Management Centre in Wrocław.
- the Minister of Infrastructure was notified that day by the President of the "Polish Waters" State Water Holding about the situation on the Odra River.
- However, it was not until 3–5 August that the Chief Inspector of Environmental Protection ordered the provincial inspectorates to determine the cause of the mass fish deaths as part of the so-called emergency monitoring. Information about the ecological disaster was received by the Minister of the Environment (also as a result of a letter from the Mayor of Oława).
- The Government Security Centre did not ask provincial crisis management centres for information on the scale of the disaster until 10 August.
- Fish sectional analyses of toxic elements, pesticides, mould toxins, persistent organic pollutant (POP) compounds and radioactive indicators did not start until 13 August.

It is worth noting that the time it takes for water to flow the entire length of the Odra River under the conditions experienced in July/August 2022 is 12 days.[120] This means that the time to take action to reduce the negative environmental effects in the event of its contamination is very short.

The course of the ecological catastrophe had two phases: the first triggered by a golden algae bloom in the lower and middle part of the river and the second also being the result of a huge amount of dead algae and fish biomass moving downstream, which caused secondary contamination.[121] Also in this context, the actions taken under conditions of uncertainty as to the causes of the disaster had a huge impact on reducing the risk during the disaster. According to the Supreme Audit Office, "the limited effectiveness of the ad hoc measures taken (by volunteers) caused the dead organic matter to move

---

[120] Free et al., 2023

[121] Czerniawski, Sługocki, 2023, p. 60–61

down the Odra River and extend the ecological disaster to further sections of the river".[122]

High fish mortality was initiated by the discharge of golden alga toxins, but the presence of this species should be limited to brackish waters,[123] and it was found upstream of a large lowland river. The very high salinity of the Odra River was exacerbated by specific weather conditions occurring with increasing frequency due to climate change.[124]

River contamination of unclear origin

The rivet-popper hypothesis[125] is very popular in the natural sciences. It compares the complexity of an ecosystem and the process of species extinction to an aeroplane that loses rivets one by one, but it is impossible to know in advance which one will prove crucial to the safety of the flight. The way to cope with this uncertainty is to take a far-reaching precautionary approach to building and implementing environmental policies and analysing details. This is because it is never possible to predict which element of the ecosystem will trigger a cascading effect in the environment, nor should its resilience to subsequent stressors ever be assumed. Uncertainty is therefore a constant.

In the social sciences, on the other hand, crisis management involves focusing on the existence of risk (in particular the possibility of predicting, estimating, analysing and reducing it) and preparing for it. The key here is not at all to seek an answer to the question "what will happen", but "what might happen", with the ideal no longer being the possibility of an event occurring, but the determination of its probability.[126] Fundamental to crisis management here, therefore, are the information held, the preventive measures taken and the response scenarios prepared.

For a long time, academic reflection on security was based on the analysis of geopolitics or armed conflicts, but for some time now, more attention has been paid to new types of threats, such as environmental pollution, loss

122 NIK, 2023, p. 19
123 Hartman et al. 2021, pp. 12–13
124 Czerniawski, Sługocki 2023, p. 6; Sun et al. 2023, p. 9
125 Ehrlih, Walker, 1998
126 Aleksandrowicz, 2023, p. 8

of biodiversity or climate change.[127] From a security perspective, all these processes are characterised by high complexity and the possibility of the occurrence of certain tipping points that can trigger large-scale, unpredictable changes. Uncertainty as to future events – as in the metaphor outlined in the rivet-popper hypothesis – is therefore a continuous state. Since these types of hazards are not linear processes, and the interrelationships between the various elements that influence them are multi-directional, cause feedbacks, and occur at all scales and in disparate systems (e.g. the environment, economy or politics), crisis management also requires a different approach. Duit and Galaz argue that for these types of crises, only a governance system that combines a high capacity for exploitation (thus providing some stability, collective actionability, decisiveness) as well as exploration (thus openness, readiness to experiment, search for new solutions, co-determination and readiness for mistakes) can cope with the task regardless of the pace of change and its predictability. In contrast, state-dominated, bureaucratic and rigid procedure-based governance seems to work best when change is slow and its predictability is high.[128]

Both the approach emphasising the need to develop analytical tools, collect information and make decisions based on verified data and the one where emphasis is on innovative solutions, accepting uncertainty and being open to mistakes prove useful in an attempt to answer the question whether it was possible to be better prepared for the Odra River crisis.

Until the second half of August, the golden alga was a species not appearing in the Polish rivers ecosystem, and certainly knowledge of its existence was not widespread. However, a significant link between this species and water salinity was already clear, and incidents of mass fish deaths due to toxin discharge had previously appeared, among others, in the UK, Denmark, the Netherlands, Israel, Germany, Hungary, the USA or China.[129] Such incidents have been mentioned regularly since the 1970s, but in Poland testing for this alga has not been systematically carried out despite widespread awareness of the high salinity of the Odra River waters due to the mining industry in Silesia. At the same time, it should be noted that in the summer of 2022,

---

[127] Burgees, 2007, pp. 67–68
[128] Duit, Galaz 2008, pp. 313–314
[129] Woźnica et al. 2024

testing for golden algae was limited only to highly specialised laboratories in Europe and there was a lack of uniform sampling and testing standards for this purpose.[130]

However, the negative impact of salt discharged into Polish rivers was no secret. It had been reported earlier by, for example, the Supreme Audit Office or the Central Mining Institute[131], and bringing rivers to a good ecological status is a fundamental objective of the Water Directive and actions taken in this area are the basis for assessing its functioning in practice.

Despite the fact that Polish law provides for the possibility of revoking a water permit for brine discharge[132] in a situation where a threat to environmental objectives has been identified, this provision appears to be dead. This is because it requires a review of water permits to assess their cumulative impact on the ecological status of the river. However, such a review has never been carried out. "The reviews conducted so far have only included an assessment of the way in which the entity concerned has exercised the powers granted in the water permits, which does not allow for a comprehensive approach to the problem of excessive water salinity. Such action by the authorities resulted from their erroneous, conservative interpretation of the applicable legislation," stated the SAO audit report.[133] At the same time, the upper chlorides and sulphates limits for wastewater are set in a regulation of the Minister of Maritime Affairs and Inland Navigation[134], but an exception is provided for discharges of highly saline waters from mining plants, which allows this limit to be exceeded if it is economically unviable or technologically impossible for a particular plant to treat its wastewater before discharge into the river[135]. Leaving aside the clear primacy of business interests over the welfare of the river ecosystem, here practice also had the decisive say for

130 Free et al. 2023

131 NIK, 1999, pp. 17–19

132 Article 136, the Water Law Act

133 NIK, 2023, p. 73

134 Currently, this department of administration has been integrated into the Ministry of Infrastructure.

135 §12(3), Regulation of the Minister of Water Management and Inland Navigation on substances particularly harmful to the aquatic environment and conditions to be met when discharging waste into surface waters or into the ground, and when discharging rainwater or snowmelt into waters or into water facilities.

possible risk reduction. The lack of possibility to treat wastewater before discharge into the river is purely declarative; it was not verified at any stage of the proceedings aimed at issuing the permit. The risk of pollution of the Odra River was not diagnosed at all.

A total of 19 hazards were included in the National Crisis Management Plan, which was in force as of March 2022, but none of them concerned surface water contamination. In the event of an incident not listed in the safety net, a decision to trigger specific actions is made based on the findings of the Government Crisis Management Team or the decision of the Prime Minister. In such a situation, however, actions in response to the Odra environmental crisis were by definition taken on the basis of ad hoc decisions. And regardless of whether these decisions were right or wrong, they were certainly overdue. Nor were threats to river water quality included in the Ministry of Infrastructure's departmental crisis management plan, even though it is the Ministry that is responsible for the administrative section "water management". In the Ministry of Environment, on the other hand, the crisis management plan was outdated and did not coincide with the actual competences of the ministry after the changes introduced in 2018. A situation adequate to the threat that occurred on the Odra River in the summer of 2022 was also not included in the provincial plans in the Śląskie, Opolskie and Dolnośląskie Provinces.[136]

Although the first information about mass fish deaths was received by the environmental inspectorate in mid-July and its specification as an ecological disaster appeared in late July and early August, until 12 August the crisis management structures and mechanisms were replaced by the work of volunteers and the Polish Angling Association. This is because anglers, as lessees of angling circuits, are normally obliged to remove dead fish from the river. Such an obligation is questionable in an environmental disaster situation; however, its recognition as such was quite fluid in the first phase of the crisis.[137]

---

136 NIK, 2023, p. 121

137 At a press conference on 10 August, Przemysław Daca, then president of Polish Waters, argued: "There are no recorded deaths of other organisms, i.e. these biological parameters are not yet so critical". On 11 August: "Our employees, but above all the Polish Angling Association, as well as volunteers, have removed at least 10 tonnes of dead fish from the river. This shows that we are dealing with a gigantic and appalling ecological disaster".

In the absence of knowledge as to the causes of the contamination of the Odra River on such a large scale, neither were the inhabitants warned of the danger nor was their access to water restricted, and in incidental cases it was even encouraged[138]. It seems that the sluggish and inconclusive response of the state was not only the result of wrong decisions, but also had its institutional basis.

Late response, diffused responsibility

The division of competences regarding the management of rivers is important for understanding the actions of the public authorities at that time. Until 2018, the administrative department of water management was subordinated to the Minister of the Environment. After a short period of existence of the Ministry of Maritime Affairs and Inland Navigation, it was incorporated into the Ministry of Infrastructure, primarily responsible for transport.

Water management, i.e., among other things, exercising ownership rights to waters, collecting fees for water services, leasing angling circuits, taking care of resources and quality of drinking water, managing waterways or counteracting droughts and floods, is the responsibility of the State Water Holding "Polish Waters" (Państwowe Gospodarstwo Wody Polskie) under the authority of the Minister of Infrastructure. However, the Minister of the Environment still supervised the Chief Inspector of Environmental Protection, an institution established to control compliance with environmental regulations and to examine and assess the state of the environment. Rivers are no exception. In addition to this, there was also a Provincial Environmental Protection Inspectorate in each province, over which the provincial governors, i.e. representatives of the government, had considerable influence. The General Director of Environmental Protection, the leading institution in matters related to the Natura 2000 network, nature protection policy and control of investment processes in terms of environmental impact assessment was also subordinate to the Minister of the Environment; this is also the second-level authority in relation to the regional directors operating

---

[138] Grzegorz Witkowski, Deputy Minister of Infrastructure, claimed at a press conference held on 11 August that he himself could enter the Odra River.

in each province. In turn, the "fishing industry" department was included in the competences of the Minister of Agriculture, who also supervised the Veterinary Inspection Service. The competences concerning the issuing of water permits and integrated permits, on the other hand, were dispersed between Polish Waters and local government units.

The Odra River during the environmental crisis was therefore the subject of attention of at least three ministries and several central authorities, and, given how long the disaster had been attributed the status of a local event, also of a number of lower-level and local government authorities in five provinces. Such a dispersion of competences is certainly not conducive to effective exchange of information and coordination of activities in an ordinary situation, while in a crisis situation the model of crisis management adopted in Poland should also be taken into account. This, too, is a multi-level model. It is made up of crisis management bodies, management centres and consultative and advisory bodies.

This is a simplified diagram of this model:

Table 1: The Crisis Management System in Poland

Level	Crisis management authority	Advisory body	Crisis Management Centre
national	Council of Ministers, Prime Minister	Government Crisis Management Team	Government Security Centre
ministerial	Minister, head of the central authority	Crisis Management Team	Crisis Management Centre
regional	governor	Provincial Crisis Management Team	Provincial Crisis Management Centre
district	head of district authorities	County Crisis Management Team	District Crisis Management Centre
municipal	commune leader, mayor, town mayor	Municipal Crisis Management Team	commune/municipal centres may or may not be established

Source: the Government Security Centre.

However, the roles assigned to the various elements of crisis management were changed or marginalised, and new solutions were introduced on an ad hoc basis.

As of 12 August, the Government Crisis Management Team dealt with the situation on the Odra River, but its function was limited to barely two recommendations[139], neither of which concerned the coordination of services or the mobilisation of forces and resources necessary to limit the effects of the crisis. The first of these concerned the establishment of an inter-ministerial coordination team to assess the situation (it was this team that took on the role of a government team and, against the law, replaced the function of departmental teams). The second was that the governors of the Lubuskie and Zachodniopomorskie provinces approached the authorities of two German states with an initiative to support the removal of dead fish from the Odra. A glaringly minor role was also played by the Government Security Centre, which was not informed about important events related to the Odra River contamination, as a result of which it itself failed to fulfil its role as a key institution responsible for the circulation of information at the national level. This resulted, among other things, in the late notification of residents about the existing threat.

According to the SAO audit, "Signals about the threat of pollution of the Odra River with a cause unknown at the initial stage had already reached the heads of the Opolskie and Dolnośląskie provinces, the State Water Holding "Polish Waters" and the authorities of the Inspectorate of Environmental Protection in July 2022. The information was sent to the Ministry of Climate and Environment and the Ministry of Infrastructure, but contrary to the rules provided for in the crisis management regulations of statutory rank, as well as in the National Crisis Management Plan, it was not communicated to the Government Security Centre."[140] The GSC was not informed of the contamination of the Odra River until late in the evening on 9 August, and this notification came from a private individual. Alerts to residents, however, were not sent until 12 August, i.e. after the Secretary of State at the Ministry of the Interior and Administration had instructed the provincial governors to intensify their activities on the Odra River. The alert was sent out precisely at the request of the heads of provincial authorities, and the first information on the environmental disaster was not officially received by the Ministry of the Interior until 11 August, among others, from the GSC. A day later, the State

[139] NIK 2023, p. 44
[140] NIK, 2023, p. 47

Fire Service, which is subordinate to the minister, was involved in the fight against the disaster in a coordinated manner. At the same time, the minister became the lead entity of the inter-ministerial team, whose formation was recommended by the Government Crisis Management Team. However, this situation lasted only until 21 August, when the Minister for the Environment and Climate became involved in leading the team as a result of a verbal order from the Prime Minister, which was not confirmed by any document. The inter-ministerial team, which in fact took on the role of coordinating the work of the services ordered to deal with the effects of the environmental disaster, thus in fact had two managers at the same time. Meetings of this team were held 22 times. Neither the Minister of the Interior nor the Minister of Infrastructure established departmental crisis management teams, and the Minister of the Environment did not convene a single such meeting in her ministry until 13 June 2023. Until he was removed from office on 16 August, the president of the State Water Holding "Polish Waters" had not appointed a crisis management team, either.

Circulation and availability of information

The duty to take crisis management action rests with the authority competent in matters of crisis management, which first received information about the occurrence of a threat. This authority immediately informs the higher and lower level authorities, respectively, about the occurrence of an incident, at the same time presenting its assessment of the situation and information on the intended actions[141]. As mentioned earlier, such information was provided in accordance with the regulation by the Mayor of Oława, who notified the provincial crisis management centre, and the President of the State Water Holding "Polish Waters", who notified the Minister of Infrastructure. However, the information about the threat was not passed on.

The circulation of information also proved to be a critical point in the next phase of the crisis management process, when coordination of activities was already taking place at the national level. Unlike before, this was no longer influenced by human error only, but also by systemic gaps and technological difficulties resulting from previous neglect.

---

141 Article 21 of the Crisis Management Act.

The Water Law Act[142] specifies that the Minister of Infrastructure, the Chief Inspector of Environmental Protection, the Chief Sanitary Inspector and the authority competent for nature conservation should conclude an agreement defining "the type, scope and manner of free provision of information necessary for activities related to monitoring and assessment of water status and water management". Such an agreement had not been concluded by the time of the Odra River crisis, which certainly made cooperation in the exchange of information to assess the ecological status of the Odra River difficult. The first problem is that the regulation does not specify which conservation authority it refers to, the second is that it omits the role of the State Water Holding "Polish Waters", as a key institution for water management. As a result, a regulation that would have had a chance to offset to some extent the negative consequences of the dispersion of responsibilities regarding the state of surface waters was not used at all.

For water management, however, the basic planning document provided for in the Water Law Act is a Water Management Plan. However, the impact of the information contained therein on the quality of the management of the Odra River crisis was negligible due to, as the SAO audit showed, "the lack of data on the progress in the implementation of the plan due to the failure to obtain annual reports from more than half of the entities obliged to implement the measures provided for in the plan".[143]As a result, the State Water Holding "Polish Waters" was unclear about what type of wastewater, in what quantities and where was discharged into the Odra River. Furthermore, this institution did not have access to analogous data resulting from the integrated permits in legal circulation, on the basis of which large-scale industrial activities are carried out. On the other hand, the information held by Polish Waters was collected in various ways: some on local servers of field units, others in the GIS system, in the form of scans in auxiliary records and even only in paper form. A similar practice was followed by the provincial inspectorates for environmental protection when collecting data on factors that could affect water quality in the Odra River basin.

Such a situation is not conducive to analysis of data required in the event of a need for a rapid response to a crisis, although it does not completely

---

142 Article 349(12), Water Law

143 NIK 2023, p. 63–64

prevent it.[144] At the time of the Odra crisis, the IT systems that were originally to be developed for the exchange and analysis of information for crisis management purposes (CAR and GISBN) were not ready to work effectively due, among other things, to a lack of funding to develop them, as a result of which the circulation of information was carried out through various channels, largely by e-mail.

Some of the crisis management activities were also not documented. For example, there was no trace of the Prime Minister's order for the Minister of the Environment to become involved in the coordination of the work of the inter-ministerial crisis management team, the subsequently declared oral order of the Secretary of State in the Ministry of Infrastructure for the Polish Waters to intensify its activities, or the ad hoc decisions taken in the initial phase of the crisis by the National Water Management Authority.

The public was also not properly informed, as the data from the water monitoring carried out by the Environmental Protection Inspectorate only started to be published on a random basis (only concerning selected parameters) in the second half of August, and the previously collected information on water quality did not make it to the Public Information Bulletin of the Ministry of the Environment and Ecology, although this would have resulted from the principles adopted in the regulations on citizens' access to information on the environment.

Conclusions. Why has the state failed to manage the crisis?

Although the SAO audit found a number of irregularities with regard to the procedures in place, this is not the only explanation for the difficulties experienced by state institutions during the crisis. After all, not all decisions were wrong, and the right ones were not always taken according to the rules. For example, it seems that the monitoring of rivers launched during the crisis and later expanded was an expected and justified action, but it does not have a proper legal basis. The inclusion of the Minister of Environment in the leadership of the inter-ministerial crisis team was contrary to the principle

[144] Balcerowska-Czerniak, Gorczyca 2024

of one-person command, and yet her activity in later weeks proved to be the only one in terms of cross-border partnership on the Odra River crisis.

Delayed, chaotic and incompatible with the principles of crisis management, the response to the Odra River crisis demonstrates a profound underestimation of a new type of threat, of which the contamination of the Odra River was only an example. Referring, once again, to the work of Duit and Galaz[145], the key features of such threats consist of the potential for seemingly insignificant events to trigger major changes, the failure to recognise all the interdependencies among the various pieces of a puzzle and their complexity, as well as the triggering of cascading effects in different areas of public policy. It follows that crisis management based on past experience cannot serve to predict the future effects of events. Public authority activities such as the Prime Minister's order to the Minister of the Environment to search for the causes of the disaster, the announcement of a reward by the Chief of Police for identifying the perpetrator of the pollution, or finally the action of the Polish Waters Authority focused on searching for illegal water devices discharging sewage into rivers were misguided actions, because they were based precisely on the assumption that since there was an unprecedented environmental crisis, its cause must have been something exceptional. And it turned out that the catastrophe had been caused by a combination of circumstances in which legal rather than illegal wastewater, discharged by state-owned companies such as mines, on the basis of permits legally issued by the state, played a major role.

The Water Directive, implemented into the Polish legal system has the following preamble: "Water is not a commercial product like any other, but rather a heritage that must be protected, defended and treated as such".[146] This objective, however, can be easily omitted in a situation where responsibilities relating to water management are dispersed among several ministries and water management, with a special emphasis on inland navigation, is subordinated to the Ministry of Infrastructure with essentially marginal powers of the Minister of the Environment. In response to the crisis, an act on the revitalisation of the Odra River was passed in July, a year after the disaster.

[145] Duit, Galaz, 2008, p. 318–323.

[146] Directive 2000/60/EC of the European Parliament and of the Council of 23 October 2000 establishing a framework for Community action in the field of water policy.

It contained dozens of investment projects favouring navigation, but not a single solution that would effectively tackle the problem of the river's salinity[147]. The systemic disregard of the latter proved to be – to borrow Ehrlich's metaphor – a critical "rivet" in the operation of public policy.

References

ALEKSANDROWICZ T., "Forecasting Threats to State Security in Theory and in Practice. Toolbox for the Analyst", *Internal Security*, 15 (1), 2023, pp. 7–8.

BALCEROWSKA- CZERNIAK G., GORCZYCA B., "Rapid assessment of surface water quality using statistical multivariate analysis approach: Odra River system case study", *Science of Total Environment*, vol. 920, 2024. <https://www.sciencedirect.com/science/article/abs/pii/S0048969723073825> access: 30 March 2025.

BURGESS J., 'Non-military security challenges', *Contemporary Security and Strategy*, 2007, pp. 67–68.

CZERNIAWSKI R., SŁUGOCKI Ł,. "Water Quality of the Odra (Odra) River before and during the Ecological Disaster in 2022: A Warning to Water Management", *Sustainability* 15 (11), 2023.

CZERNIAWSKI Robert, SŁUGOCKI Łukasz. (2023 b). 'Lessons from the Odra environmental disaster', *Academia, the magazine of Polish Academy of Science* 2 (78).

DUIT A., GALAZ V. "Governance and Complexity—Emerging Issues for Governance Theory", *Governance* 21 (3), 2008, pp. 313–326.

EHRLICH P., WALKER B., 'Rivets and Redundancy', *BioScience 48(5), 1998*, pp. 387–388.

FREE Garry. et al., "Climate change and ecological assessment in Europe under the WFD – Hitting moving targets with shifting baselines?", *Journal of Environmental Management*, vol. 370, 2024, <https://www.sciencedirect.com/science/article/pii/S0301479724028706>, access: 25 March 2025.

[147] Fees for brine discharges into the Odra River were increased only symbolically and postponed, and its retention was ordered for barely a few days.

FREE G. et al., “An EU analysis of the ecological disaster in the Odra River of 2022”, *Joint Research Centre European Commission*, 2023, <https://op.europa.eu/en/publication-detail/-/publication/acae85a4-ae18-11ed-8912-01aa75ed71a1/language-en>, access: 24 March 2025.

HARTMAN K. J. et al., ‘A Case Study of a Prymnesium parvum Harmful Algae Bloom in the Ohio River Drainage: Impact, Recovery and Potential for Future Invasions/Range Expansion’ *Water*, 13(22), 2021, pp. 12–13.

NAJWYŻSZA IZBA KONTROLI, „Informacja o wynikach kontroli realizacji opłat za zasolenie wód powierzchniowych i emisję dwutlenku siarki”, 1999, <https://www.nik.gov.pl/kontrole/wyniki-kontroli-nik/kontrole,400.html> access: 30 March 2025.

NAJWYŻSZA IZBA KONTROLI, „Działania podmiotów publicznych w związku z kryzysem ekologicznym na rzece Odrze”, 2023. https://www.nik.gov.pl/aktualnosci/odra-kryzys-ekologiczny.html access: 15 March 2025.

SUN J. et al.,”Long-term daily water temperatures unveil escalating water warming and intensifying heatwaves in the Odra River Basin, Central Europe”, *Geoscience Frontiers* 15 (6), 2024, p. 9.

SZLAUER- ŁUKASZEWSKA A. et al., “Quantifying a mass mortality event in freshwater wildlife within the Lower Odra River: Insights from a large European river”, *Science of Total Environment*, vol. 907, 2024, <https://www.sciencedirect.com/science/article/abs/pii/S0048969723065257>, access: 28 March 2025.

WOŹNICA A. et al. ‘The reaction of Prymnesium parvum to a sudden salinity decrease’, Ecohydrology& Hydrobiology, 2024. https://www.sciencedirect.com/science/article/pii/S1642359324001071, access: 15 March 2025.

Data Management in Local Government Units in Poland: Challenges and Issues in the 21st Century

Grzegorz Haber[148]

ABSTRACT
The digital transformation of public administration in Poland has highlighted the critical importance of effective data management in local government units (LGUs). As these institutions are responsible for managing vast amounts of data related to public services, urban planning, and civic engagement, the need for modernised and secure data practices has become paramount. This paper examines the specific challenges faced by Polish LGUs in the 21st century, including legal and regulatory obligations, data privacy, and cybersecurity. The study explores how emerging technologies, such as big data, artificial intelligence, and cloud computing, can be leveraged to improve the efficiency and transparency of public administration. Additionally, the paper addresses the practical difficulties of implementing new data management systems in the context of limited financial resources and human capital. By focusing on the unique circumstances of Poland's decentralised local governance model, the article offers an in-depth analysis of current trends and future directions in data management, proposing solutions that are tailored to the needs of Polish LGUs.

Keywords: data management, local government unit, Poland, crisis management

Introduction

Public administration in the 21st century uses more and more digital data as a key resource in its operations. It should be noted that orientation towards new technologies is not pointwise or directly dependent on the implementation of a newly discovered invention, but is one of the processes that individual organisational units need to manage effectively. Digital assets, i.e. data, are subject to many different activities, including aggregation, processing and use. At each stage, difficulties pile up, which, for public management, make an interesting contribution to multi-faceted research.

Historically, data have been the focus of public administration. The first traces of their use can be seen in antiquity, where useful information for

148 Dr Grzegorz Haber - University of Opole, Assistant Professor, Department of Governance and Public Policy, ORCID: 0000-0002-6094-2492.

specific communities was recorded on clay plaques, which could serve as a reference point for economic, political, but also cultural and even sporting activities. The first registers obviously did not have a structured form, but as more data were created and collected, a natural need to come up with a way of organising them and putting them into a proper form appeared. It can be assumed that some of the first successful attempts to implement empire-wide data management systems were made in the Roman Empire. Already the emperor-philosopher Marcus Aurelius pointed out the most important challenge: "The activities of things are in constant change, and the causes work in infinite varieties; and there is hardly anything which stands still"[149]. With reference to these words, in which the need to accept variability and to constantly respond to changing circumstances is highlighted, it is worth noting the importance of the challenges of the first administrative organisms, as the experiences gathered at that time provided a reference point for deliberations on good administrative systems in the modern period, as well as for the creators of bureaucratic systems that used data to efficiently manage states at the turn of the 20th century[150]. What distinguishes modern states from historical cases is above all the availability of data in the digital space, which has happened as a result of the coupling of several processes: the emergence of new information technologies (e.g. the intranet, internet and generative artificial intelligence), technological resources in the form of equipment to process and use data (e.g. computers, server rooms, machine databases), but also the massification of education, the increasing significance of civil society and changing paradigms of people's functioning in the modern age. It is clear that the era we live in is one of coexistence between people and technology, where data constitute a key resource for all actors in our communities.

From the point of view of public administration, including local government units, information has become a strategic resource. Datasets make it possible to make decisions at every level of the functioning of the official structure, in which the elements of the system are not only officials and the office as a superior entity, but also citizens, businesses and NGOs. Also

---

[149] M. Aurelius, *Rozmyślania*, translated by Marian Reiter, Wydawnictwo Etiuda, Kraków 2024, p. 88.

[150] D. Reid, "Reading Fayol with 3d glasses", *Journal of Management History*, 1(3), 1996, pp. 63–71 https://doi.org/10.1108/13552529510095143

important in the operating structure is a matrix showing cooperation with other offices, which in practice consists in the transfer of digital data in an appropriate form, e.g. between municipalities when they jointly manage the issue of municipal waste, or between local authorities and a composite administration, e.g. in the event of various crises and disasters, but also in day-to-day operations, e.g. with tax administration authorities on tax issues.

In Poland, the process of implementing data management is sometimes equated with digitisation and an attempt to adapt to the patterns disseminated at various times by the European Union. Hence numerous programmes and competitions to adapt to the digital world: "Digital Municipality" financed by European Funds[151], the development of digital services within the concept of "Integrated State Informatisation"[152], or the various modules within the National Reconstruction Plan[153]. Various digital components were purchased, staff was trained and data banks were equipped to process information in the best possible way. Over the years, it is difficult to discern a clear-cut path to follow based on a baseline model of the digital world, as new ideas and concepts have emerged along with the changing governments in Poland, which is well illustrated by the provisions of the "Integrated State Informatisation" concept, which will be updated and adapted to the emerging concept of resilience to threats in the near future[154]. This state of affairs has resulted in a number of barriers to development in this area in Poland: competence gaps among officials and citizens; disparities in digital infrastructure across the country, with particular reference to the difference in the wealth of individual local government units; and low responsiveness to crisis challenges due to the resources held by the units concerned. In times of contemporary challenges, it becomes important to highlight the need for urgent action on data management in this dimension.

The objective of this paper is to analyse the challenges faced by local government units in Poland in managing data in the reality of the 21st century.

---

151 *Digital Poland Projects Centre*, Digital Municipality project. https://www.gov.pl/web/cppc/cyfrowa-gmina

152 *Integrated State Informatisation Programme*. https://www.gov.pl/web/ia/program-zintegrowanej-cyfryzacji-panstwa,

153 *National Reconstruction Plan*. https://www.kpo.gov.pl/strony/o-kpo/o-kpo/informacje/

154 C. Aradau, "The promise of security: resilience, surprise and epistemic politics", *Resilience*, 2:2, 2014, pp. 73–87. DOI: 10.1080/21693293.2014.914765

The research carried out focuses on the diagnosis of practices and perceptions of the importance and overarching values in the data management process from an institutional and technological perspective. For the purposes of this paper, particular emphasis is placed on highlighting the use of data in the context of public emergency management. The specific research questions are therefore the following: What are the main problems and challenges regarding data management in LGUs?; What practices and solutions in this area are used in Polish local governments?; and How are data used in decision-making processes and in dealing with potential crisis activities at the local level? A query of the results of similar projects was used to prepare the research, and theoretical accounts of data management challenges were analysed. As a result of the preliminary work carried out, it was decided to present the results of the quantitative research conducted by means of an online survey, in which questions on the following problems and challenges with data management were sent to all LGUs. Additionally, a case study of the preparation of two editions of the Opole city development strategy, in which the author of this paper had the pleasure to participate, is presented.

A theoretical approach to data management

In 2015, the Organisation for Economic Co-operation and Development published a report entitled *Data-Driven Innovation. Big Data for Growth and Well-Being*, which represents a milestone in the discussion on how to define data management in a digital world. The document outlines the impact of the process of widespread access to data on various aspects of the economy, politics and society. The ten chapters offer an analysis of specific ways to derive additional value from an effective way of managing data at different levels. Particularly noteworthy is Chapter 9 ("Cities as hubs for data-driven innovation") and Chapter 10 ("Governments leading by example with public sector data"), which provide an interesting reference point for reflections on the quality of data management in local government units. At the same time, the authors use the definition of *data governance*, pointing out the key factors in the process of good data governance: open access and reusability of data, data interoperability (i.e. recording data in forms that allow them to be easily processed), combining data into larger sets (e.g. through the use of data banks) and drawing attention to public ownership and data value[155]. This was the first such a comprehensive study to draw attention to the need to include the idea of proper data management in the process of building cities of the future, which came to be known as *Smart Cities*[156].

Non-governmental organisations play an important role in the dissemination of knowledge of data management in local government units. A good example is the work of the Institute for Urban and Regional Development, which, as part of the Observatory on Urban and Regional Policy, produced a handbook for local authorities[157]. A validation sheet was prepared when working on materials for local authorities, which was used by individual LGUs to determine compliance with the proposed template. Strong emphasis in the handbook is placed on how to obtain and share data, which can contribute to their effective use in the implementation of various public policies within the city. The authors of the Institute for Urban and Regional Development handbook attach great importance to a set of good practices that enable local government units to organise data well, e.g. using tools such as the urban lab, which are meant to become "an instrument of cooperation between local authorities and citizens, enterprises and scientific entities, aiming to improve the quality of life through innovative solutions to identified problems and to generate additional value using urban resources"[158].

Data management by administrative units was the subject of research and academic consideration in the past. The focus was both on the technical aspects, i.e. primarily the methods and processing of information, but also on a number of specific issues, including open access to data, knowledge management in administration, and the efficiency of public administration activities. Interesting in this context is the research of Gye-Soo Kim, carried out in South Korea, which illuminates the relationship in this respect between the public and private spheres. This is particularly important when business

---

[155] OECD (2015), *Data-Driven Innovation: Big Data for Growth and Well-Being*, OECD Publishing, Paris. *http://dx.doi.org/10.1787/9789264229358-en*

[156] S. Baraniewicz-Kotasińska, „Smart city. Four approaches to the concept of understanding", *Urban Research & Practice*, 2020. DOI: 10.1080/17535069.2020.1818817

[157] W. Łachowski, K. Janas, *Introduction* [in W. Łachowski, 2021, *Data management in cities. Handbook for Local Governments*], Kraków-Warszawa 2021, IRMiR Press, http://obserwatorium.miasta.pl/wp-content/uploads/2021/10/IRMiR_Zarzadzaniedanymi_20210922-4.pdf

[158] Ibidem, p. 179.

has a significant technological advantage in this field and, in its actions, in a way forces the process of public administration's adaptation to the new reality. Gye-Soo Kim's research pays particular attention to the issue of quality management as a key focal point, where other elements including big data and effective leadership have a crucial impact on the actual improvement of public services[159]. A different perspective is adopted by a team of Indonesian researchers led by Budi Gunawan, for whom the most relevant process is digital transformation and its effectiveness in the context of collaboration with citizens-users at different levels of interaction, including, most notably, the adoption and sharing of information[160]. It is clear that the research perspective is determined by the local conditions that individual researchers deal with. This is important because they operate with diverse resources, differing considerably in the case of South Korea and Indonesia.

In Poland, the topic of data management in LGUs is a relatively new field of research and is mainly emphasised in studies on the organisational efficiency of administrative local government units. In this context, data become a key resource for making right decisions, whether in current situations, as in the case of research conducted by Maria Jastrzębska, for whom data are the primary source of LGUs' effectiveness[161], or in emergency situations such as the COVID-19 pandemic, where individual LGUs had to respond appropriately to minimise its impact on the functioning of the whole community. The research carried out by Elżbieta Ociepa-Kicińska and her team brings a lot of valuable insights into the quality of data and the hindered use of data to assess the dynamically changing situation of LGUs[162].

---

159 G. Kim, "The effect of quality management and big data management on customer satisfaction in Korea's public sector", *Sustainability*, 12(13), 2020, p. 5474. https://doi.org/10.3390/su12135474

160 B. Gunawan, B. Ratmono, P., Setyoko, "Digital transformation in public management functions for public information disclosure", *Journal of Governance*, 8(3), 2023. https://doi.org/10.31506/jog.v8i3.20451

161 M. Jastrzębska, "The conditions of measuring local government units expenditure efficiency", *Zeszyty Naukowe Uniwersytetu Szczecińskiego Finanse Rynki Finansowe Ubezpieczenia*, 6, 2016, pp. 43–53. https://doi.org/10.18276/frfu.2016.84/1-04

162 E.Ociepa-Kicińska, M. Gorzałczyńska-Koczkodaj, K. Brzozowska, P. Pluskota, "An assessment of the financial condition of local government units in view of the covid-19 pandemic as exemplified by self-governing provinces in Poland", *Regional Development and Policy*, (59), 2022. https://doi.org/10.14746/rrpr.2022.59.10

Results of the quantitative research

In order to obtain information on the relevance and importance of the perception of data management issues by LGUs in Poland a survey was carried out using a digital tool in the period from May to September 2024. An invitation to participate in the survey was sent by e-mail to all LGUs in Poland and 233 correctly verified responses were received. The questionnaire comprised a set of closed and open-ended questions, so that respondents were also able to provide their own free statements. The survey was exploratory in nature, and the author's objective was to provide a broad diagnosis of the situation, along with an identification of the most important challenges and problems related to data management in Polish local government units, and therefore making maximum use of the multiple-choice option or the possibility to add one's own suggestions was important. It is noteworthy that different types of units took part in the survey: municipalities, city halls, district authority offices and marshal offices. A breakdown by the type of unit and province that took part in the survey is shown in the table below:

Table 1: LGUs participating in the survey

Province	Municipal Office	City Hall	District Authority Office	Marshal's Office
Dolnośląskie	5	5	1	
Kujawsko-Pomorskie	8	4	3	1
Lubelskie	5	6	3	
Lubuskie	2	1		
Łódzkie	9	4	5	
Małopolskie	15	10	5	1
Mazowieckie	15	4	1	1
Opolskie	5	3	1	
Podkarpackie	10	2	2	1
Podlaskie	2	6	1	
Pomorskie	3	3	1	
Śląskie	11	11	2	
Świętokrzyskie	7	6	4	
Warmińsko-Mazurskie	7	7		
Wielkopolskie	11	6	1	
Zachodniopomorskie	4	1	1	

The percentage of individual units in the survey with regard to their representativeness against the types and provinces concerned was mostly maintained. The extreme results are puzzling, i.e. an insignificant participation of LGUs from Lubuskie Province and an above-average participation of LGUs from Kujawsko-Pomorskie Province.

A question was asked about the thematic data sets processed in the LGUs and the top three included:

1. Infrastructure data (228 confirmations)
2. Spatial planning data (217)
3. Environmental data (214)

It is interesting to note that the data sets indicated the least frequently were those relating to employment (87 confirmations) and health (69 confirmations).

In terms of technical solutions, LGUs indicated that they used spreadsheets (164 confirmations), as well as commercial systems for management (e.g. EZD, SAP, Oracle – 81), open source systems (40) and internally developed systems (60). However, a large number of participants ticked the option of *no special solutions* (as many as 91), which shows a great deal of variation in terms of the very way in which data are managed at a particular unit level. Significantly, no correlation was shown either at the geographical level or at the level of the type of LGU, which may indicate a deeper dimension of the issue that should be explored further in a subsequent study. This is particularly important in the context of responses obtained to the question on *data management procedures and policies* implemented in the office. For this question, a fairly clear picture was obtained:

Table 2: Answers to question 5: *What data management procedures and policies have been implemented in the office?*

Answer	Number of indications
Data security procedures (e.g. encryption, backups)	231
Data access procedures (e.g. rights to view and modify data)	206
Data security audits	201
Data management training for employees	195
Data storage procedures (e.g. locally, in a cloud)	167

It is worth noting that the answers were prepared on the basis of the *good practices* identified in the Urban and Regional Development handbook and are also reflected in the legal requirements for the functioning of individual LGUs[163]. Thus, at the operational level, the data are properly secured and the performed activities connected with them are carried out based on existing procedures, but the management methods are very different. This duality in the functioning of the LGUs can be seen well in the answers obtained to the question in which the respondents were asked to rank the activities related to the use of data from the most important to the least important one.

Table 3: Answers to question 6: *How does the office use the data collected?*

Activity	Place in global ranking	W1 (%)	W2 (%)	W3 (%)	W4 (%)	W5 (%)	W6 (%)	W7 (%)	W8 (%)	W9 (%)	W10 (%)
Planning	1.	43	24	14	5	6	5	2	0	1	0
Analysis	2.	29	38	17	7	3	3	2	1	0	0
Monitoring	3.	6	17	42	17	5	5	5	2	0	0
Reporting	4.	4	6	11	45	15	6	5	6	2	0
Management	5.	14	6	5	5	6	11	41	10	2	0
Archiving	6.	2	2	2	6	40	17	8	7	6	9
Making available	7.	0	2	5	5	13	44	13	9	5	4
Production of statistics	8.	0	0	2	3	5	3	13	51	16	8
Cooperation with other entities	9.	1	3	2	4	4	5	8	9	55	10
Process improvement	10.	0	0	1	4	3	2	4	5	12	69

[163] W. Łachowski, K. Janas, Introduction [in W. Łachowski, 2021, Data management in cities. Handbook for Local Governments], Kraków - Warszawa 2021, IRMiR Press, http://obserwatorium.miasta.pl/wp-content/uploads/2021/10/IRMiR_Zarzadzaniedanymi_20210922-4.pdf

Specialised activities being indicated in the first place, followed by sharing or process improvement – the key activities from our perspective of management – is an interesting phenomenon. The particularly low percentage of indications concerning the use of collected data to ensure office efficiency is an interesting point of reference requiring further research. Particularly, because when asked about *the main objectives of data management by the office*, the respondents ranked improving the efficiency of the administration in the second place. Only ensuring compliance was placed higher, which may indicate a problem related to the divergence between the desired objective and the possibilities of actually achieving it. The authorities would like the processed data to contribute to making the administration more efficient, but this state of affairs is not achievable.

Among the perceived challenges in data management, LGUs provided very diverse answers:

Table 4: Answers to question 8: *What challenges does the office face in terms of data management?*

Challenge	Number of responses
Financial constraints	165
Changing legal regulations	130
Limited staff resources	124
Problems with integration of different information systems	92
Difficulty in adapting to new technologies	55
Data security issues	53
Lack of data management training for employees	28
Lack of technical support	28
Difficulties in archiving and storing data	17

It is not surprising that financial constraints were perceived as a key challenge in data management. On the other hand, it is also worth noting the issues of changing legal regulations and staff constraints. It is evident that technical (technological) challenges, which could be competently made up for, for example through training, are not treated as key challenges and hence the efficiency of dealing with them is potentially high. Simultaneously, the perception of challenges faced by local government units in Poland (with their limited power of action in this area as they operate within the framework of laws enacted at the central level) as those of key importance raises a number of issues and further challenges that individual offices will face in the future appear.

The research clearly shows a picture of administrative units implementing numerous data management-related activities and measures, despite numerous challenges and problems. Potential barriers that came to light in the study, such as limited financial and human resources, are extremely difficult to overcome with little support from the central state administration at the financial as well as organisational level. The respondents also pointed to the challenge concerning problems with integrating different IT systems, arguing that each office used many types of software serving different purposes. The lack of integration across a given office and also across the state administration maximises the risk of management difficulties in crisis situations, where time is an extremely important resource[164].

Case study: preparation of strategic development documents for the city of Opole on the basis of available data

Planning was selected as one of the key data management activities in the quantitative survey results by the respondents from LGUs. One of its most important elements is certainly reliance on strategic documents in day-to-day operations; the most relevant of these documents being *The Development Strategy*. The author of this paper was invited to work as an expert on the edition of the strategy for the period until 2030 and is now involved in the preparation of the strategy covering the subsequent years until 2043[165]. In the process of preparing the document, the staff resources of the Opole City Hall were used, but numerous people from the external environment were also invited: scientists, representatives of the world of culture, art and sports;

[164] B. Wiśniewski, B. Kaczmarczyk, "Opportunity, Challenge, Risk and Threat — Review of Definitions and Relations", *Internal Security*, 9 (2), 2017, pp. 23–32. https://doi.org/10.5604/01.3001.0012.1699

[165] *Strategy of Development of the City of Opole to 2030*. https://www.opole.pl/sites/default/files/field_attachment/2020-02/Strategia%20Rozwoju.pdf

the document was consulted with residents and businesspeople as well as non-governmental organisations.

Work on the 2030 edition was divided into 10 thematic working groups, responsible for the various area of urban activity (Civic Opole; sport and tourism; infrastructure, public transport, cycle paths; business, innovation, entrepreneurship, science; social policy, senior citizen policy, family, health; education; spatial planning and architecture; green areas and environmental protection; culture and promotion; and smart administration). The substantive scope of the strategy renders well the social climate and civic spirit at the end of the second decade of the 21st century, as reflected in the final version of the document, adopted by the Opole City Council on 29 August 2019.

Work on the document lasted several months and each of the experts had the opportunity to review the input data prepared by the City Hall staff. These included, among other things, demographic data, which made it possible to plan the distribution of emphasis appropriately to social groups in view of their potential size (adolescents, young adults, seniors, etc.), detailed data on social and technical infrastructure and numerous discussions with officials about the economic and institutional conditions at the time, as well as many forecasts and trends for the future. A SWOT analysis was also carried out, where numerous empirical data were used.

The management of input data and the organisation of the work on its effective use were carried out within individual working groups. Subsequently, representatives of the City Hall collected baseline data and prepared target recommendations, on the basis of which *The Development Strategy of the City of Opole until 2030* was edited. Consultations with residents and community groups followed and a process of formal adoption of the document, by way of a resolution of the City Council, was planned.

The data management process itself in all its elements should be assessed as effective. Referring to the classic CRISP-DM model, one could see a fluid transition between the successive phases of the process from understanding the situation through preparing data packages to modelling and implementing the target solution[166]. The process used the available resources – external

[166] J. Brzozowska, J. Pizoń, A. Gola, A. Zakimova, K. Piotrowska, "Data engineering in crisp-dm process production data – a case study", *Management Science*, 19 (3), 2023, pp. 83–95 https://doi.org/10.35784/acs-2023-26

experts had the knowledge and skills to participate in the work of the various teams. It is worth noting that the strategy development process was carried out "in-house", without the use of external entities, which meant that the final form and content of the document, consulted and adopted by the City Council, is still up-to-date and can be effectively used in the current activities by the Opole City Hall.

Taking into account the experience gained at the previous edition, the City of Opole, while preparing for the work on *The Development Strategy until 2043*, decided to prepare *A Diagnosis of the Situation of the City of Opole*, which is a document analysing previous activities, directly resulting from the current city development strategy, but also signalling current problems and challenges. Importantly, *A Diagnosis* was published on the Public Information Bulletin website, so that every resident could have access to it already at the stage of collecting data for the preparation of a new strategy[167]. Two changes at this stage are worth noting. New analytical tools and resources were used to analyse data, which indicated the office's process of continuous adaptation to new technological challenges, and new scopes of data were proposed, enriched with, among other things, data on climate change. *A Diagnosis* is an important planning and strategic document that is a bank of key data for the city. It includes not only a description of the current state or monitoring of the implementation of *The Development Strategy to 2030*, but above all an analysis of the city development conditions and the state of the city development. For analysts and researchers, as well as for all those interested in the development of LGUs, this is certainly a viable and key reference point for work on urban reality.

The new strategy is still being developed and is still in the data collection and processing stage, with the support of external experts and numerous community groups, but it is clear that data are the key resource for formulating objectives, activities to be carried out or the baseline parts of the document itself. Thus, we have an interesting case study in which the previous edition of activities is not only a point of reference, but is being supplemented with new elements. It is worth noting here, first and foremost, the security

---

167 Diagnosis of the situation of the City of Opole developed for the process of preparing the Opole Development Strategy until 2043. https://www.bip.um.opole.pl/uploaded_files/serwis_files/attachments/bip/5822/e0307a54f0895c97.pdf

perspective and the desire to create a document with a much longer time span than the previous version.

Conclusions

Data management in local government units is becoming one of the key challenges of modern public administration, taking into account external conditions (a security policy and the need for effective emergency responses), but also internal ones, which are related to the coexistence of numerous processes of adaptation to the expectations of residents and the capabilities of offices and office staff. Data, not just as a confirmation and record of facts, but more as a strategic and key resource to analyse, plan and manage organisations and numerous public policies, gain a much greater significance. This happens through a constant process of adaptation, where both authorities and residents react to each other's actions. In this sequence of changes, the main objective of the functioning of public administration, which in the 21st century is to effectively manage a variety of processes using very limited human and financial resources, must not disappear. Preparing local government units not only to respond, but above all to manage a crisis situation efficiently, requires not only the development of new procedures, which is more related to the need to make proper use of the data held by individual local government units, yet managing them is very difficult.

The quantitative survey provided a better understanding of how local government units in Poland approach data management and what challenges they face. The answers received clearly indicate that the level of advancement in this field depends on the resources available and on the changing circumstances. Among the numerous challenges, those which are beyond the control of LGUs and which require changes at the central level were primarily indicated, i.e. the lack of staff resources is largely related to the state's fiscal policy and the co-existence of numerous data collection and processing systems is not coordinated at the central level, which causes numerous difficulties also at the level of the organisation of local authorities. As an example of a good practice in the use of data, the paper presents the preparation of a development strategy by the city of Opole, a process that illustrates effective data management by local government units in Poland.

The findings gathered in the research process allow a number of recommendations and guidelines to be formulated that are worth considering in data management processes, but also in future scientific projects. Firstly, attention should be paid to the strong development of competences of local government staff to use data in operational processes. The analysis of the questionnaires indicates that further development of competency is desirable, but a major barrier is the lack of coordination at the level of LGUs and the central government. It would be advisable to emphasise the need for a stronger centralisation of data management processes, which could greatly facilitate the functioning of smaller units in particular. Secondly, the idea of open data and making data available to citizens and community groups should be further developed and managed effectively. As the example of data exchange between the office and experts in the context of preparing the Opole city development strategy shows, it is possible to achieve a satisfactory result with limited resources. Thirdly, the interoperability of resources, including technology and infrastructure, should be subjected to cyclical evaluation processes. Data management shows well that at the level of legislation, e.g. GDPR or the EU *Digital Data Act*, the theoretical approach must be closely linked to the practical implementation. The constant intermingling of data which are or may be in the possession of a given LGU is associated with numerous organisational and technical difficulties, but it is worth overcoming them, as taking care of their proper use is crucial for building the organisational efficiency of every local government in Poland.

References

ARADAU C., "The promise of security: resilience, surprise and epistemic politics", *Resilience*, 2:2, 2014, pp. 73–87. DOI: 10.1080/21693293.2014.914765

AURELIUS M., *Rozmyślania*, translated by Marian Reiter, Wydawnictwo Etiuda, Kraków 2024.

BARANIEWICZ-KOTASIŃSKA S., „Smart city. Four approaches to the concept of understanding", *Urban Research & Practice*, 2020. DOI: 10.1080/17535069.2020.1818817

BRZOZOWSKA, J., PIZOŃ, J., GOLA, A., ZAKIMOVA, A., & PIOTROWSKA, K., "Data engineering in crisp-dm process production data – a case study", *Management Science*, 19(3), 2023, pp. 83–95. https://doi.org/10.35784/acs-2023-26

Diagnosis of the situation of the City of Opole developed for the process of preparing the Opole Development Strategy until 2043. https://www.bip.um.opole.pl/uploaded_files/serwis_files/attachments/bip/5822/e0307a54f0895c97.pdf

Digital Poland Projects Centre, Digital Municipality project. https://www.gov.pl/web/cppc/cyfrowa-gmina

Integrated State Informatisation Programme. https://www.gov.pl/web/ia/program-zintegrowanej-cyfryzacji-panstwa

JASTRZĘBSKA, M., "The conditions of measuring local government units expenditure efficiency", *Zeszyty Naukowe Uniwersytetu Szczecińskiego Finanse Rynki Finansowe Ubezpieczenia*, 6, 2016, pp. 43–53. https://doi.org/10.18276/frfu.2016.84/1-04

GUNAWAN, B., RATMONO, B., & SETYOKO, P., "Digital transformation in public management functions for public information disclosure", *Journal of Governance*, 8(3), 2023. https://doi.org/10.31506/jog.v8i3.20451

KIM, G., "The effect of quality management and big data management on customer satisfaction in Korea's public sector". *Sustainability*, 12(13), 2020, p. 5474. https://doi.org/10.3390/su12135474

ŁACHOWSKI W., JANAS K., 2021, *Introduction* [in W. Łachowski, 2021, *Data management in cities. Handbook for Local Governments*], Kraków-Warszawa 2021, IRMiR Press. http://obserwatorium.miasta.pl/wp-content/uploads/2021/10/IRMiR_Zarzadzaniedanymi_20210922-4.pdf

OCIEPA-KICIŃSKA, E., GORZAŁCZYŃSKA-KOCZKODAJ, M., BRZOZOWSKA, K., & PLUSKOTA, P., An assessment of the financial condition of local government units in view of the covid-19 pandemic as exemplified by self-governing provinces in Poland. Regional Development and Policy, (59), 2022. https://doi.org/10.14746/rrpr.2022.59.10

OECD (2015), Data-Driven Innovation: Big Data for Growth and Well-Being, OECD Publishing, Paris 2015. http://dx.doi.org/10.1787/9789264229358-en

National Reconstruction Plan. https://www.kpo.gov.pl/strony/o-kpo/o-kpo/informacje/

REID, D., Reading Fayol with 3d glasses. Journal of Management History, 1(3), 2012, pp. 63–71. https://doi.org/10.1108/13552529510095143

Strategy of Development of the City of Opole to 2030. https://www.opole.pl/sites/default/files/field_attachment/2020-02/Strategia%20Rozwoju.pdf

WIŚNIEWSKI, B., & KACZMARCZYK, B., Opportunity, Challenge, Risk and Threat — Review of Definitions and Relations. Internal Security, 9(2), 2017, pp. 23–32. https://doi.org/10.5604/01.3001.0012.1699

The use of social media by local authorities in crisis situations: evidence from the 2024 flood in Nysa

Sabina Baraniewicz-Kotasińska[168]

ABSTRACT

Effective communication is a critical component of ensuring public safety during crisis situations. The advent and widespread adoption of social media have transformed the landscape of crisis communication. Social media platforms enable rapid, interactive, and wide-reaching communication, offering new opportunities for public officials to engage directly with affected communities. Despite growing scholarly interest in this field, questions remain regarding the expectations of residents and the efficacy of social media use by city authorities during emergencies. This study addresses these gaps by examining the use of social media for crisis communication by the mayor of Nysa, Kordian Kolbiarz, during the September 2024 flood. Through a case study of content published on the mayor's official Facebook page, this chapter investigates the types of information expected by residents, the effectiveness of social media communication strategies employed by local authorities, and the advantages and limitations of these platforms usage during crisis. The findings contribute to a deeper understanding of the role social media can play in enhancing public communication and engagement during emergencies.

Keywords: crisis communication, social media, local authorities, flood

Introduction

In a crisis situation, an integral element of ensuring the safety of the population is effective communication with both internal and external environments[169]. Hitherto, the primary channels for mass communication during a crisis were traditional media, such as print, radio, and television. With the advent of the internet, this space has naturally expanded to include new sources of communication.

---

[168] Dr Sabina Baraniewicz-Kotasińska, University of Opole, Assistant Professor, Department of Governance and Public Policy, ORCID: 0000-0002-3545-6206.

[169] B. Kosowski, A. Luzar A, *Potencjał wykorzystania mediów społecznościowych w sytuacjach kryzysowych - zarys problemu*, in: *Prasa lokalna i samorządowa: propozycje zmian legislacyjnych*, edited by A. Gołębiowska, P. B. Zientarski, Szkoła Główna Służby Pożarniczej, Warszawa 2020, pp. 125–136.

Social media has assumed a particularly important role in crisis communication, as it, free from the limitations of traditional media, enables the rapid publication of content and dynamic information exchange, including interaction with the audience[170]. Its popularity and widespread use have led leaders to increasingly turn to these highly dynamic communication tools to disseminate important information among their followers[171].

With the rise of social media as an alternative to traditional communication media, researchers have begun to explore the various ways in which social media are used to communicate during times of crisis. In general, researchers have found that public officials can leverage the ubiquity and penetration of social media to spread messages farther and faster than would be possible with traditional media[172].

Despite the extensive discussion of this topic in academic literature, much is still unknown about the role social media play in disseminating information during critical events. The aim of this research is to further explore this issue.

This chapter examines the issue of social media use by city authorities for communication with residents during a crisis. The author's primary focus is to identify the advantages and disadvantages of using social media for crisis communication, as well as to highlight key elements that should be considered when employing these platforms for such purposes. The author has formulated three research questions:

1. What kind of information do individuals affected by a crisis expect during a critical situation?
2. How should effective crisis communication by city authorities be conducted through social media?
3. What are the advantages and disadvantages of using social media for communication purposes during a crisis?

---

170 Ibidem.

171 J. Jr London, K. Matthews, "Crisis communication on social media - lessons from Covid-19", *Journal of Decision Systems*, vol. 31, no. 1–2, 2021, pp. 150–170. DOI: https://doi.org/10.1080/12460125.2021.1926612

172 J. Sutton, C. B. Gibson, E. S. Spiro, C. League, S. M. Fitzhugh, C. T. Butts, "What it takes to get passed on: Message content, style, and structure as predictors of retransmission in the Boston marathon bombing response", *PLoS ONE*, vol. 10, no. 8, 2015. DOI: https://doi.org/10.1371/journal.pone.0134452

This research problem is analyzed through the case study of crisis communication by the mayor of Nysa, Kordian Kolbiarz, with the residents of the Nysa municipality during the flood that occurred in September 2024. The study focuses on the mayor's official Facebook page, specifically the announcements and comments posted on his profile during the period of emerging risk and throughout the crisis. The analyzed timeframe spans from September 12 to September 18, 2024.

Crisis Communication with the use of social media – theoretical background

In a crisis situation, the efficient flow of information is a key element in fostering a sense of security within the community[173]. A crisis is generally defined as an unusual, significant, and public situation that leads to highly negative consequences for those affected (Coombs 2007). Some crises are short-lived and quickly resolved, while others, such as floods, famine, or pandemics, can last for extended periods.

During crises, public officials increasingly utilize social media as a communication tool to engage with citizens. These platforms enable them to provide timely updates, share critical information, and offer guidance to the public in moments of heightened uncertainty and distress[174]. By using social media, officials can directly engage with citizens, address concerns in real time, and foster a sense of transparency and trust[175]. This shift reflects the growing recognition of digital platforms as essential for crisis communication, allowing for rapid dissemination of information without the constraints of traditional media channels.

Social media has become an essential component of contemporary political communication and governance in general. As pointed out by Jungherr, "modern political leaders are much more reliant on social media platforms as tools for communicating with voters, announcing legislation and casting

173 B. Kosowski, A. Luzar A, *op. cit.*

174 J. London, K. Matthews, *op. cit.*

175 B. Kosowski, *Komunikacja ze społeczeństwem w zarządzaniu sytuacjami kryzysowymi*, in: *Państwo, gospodarka, społeczeństwo w integrującej się Europie*, edited by Klemens Budzowski, Krakowskie Towarzystwo Edukacyjne, Kraków 2003, pp. 191–202.

vision"[176]. Moreover, the overall function of social media has evolved, serving not only as a space for social interaction but also as a vital tool for real-time information dissemination and response to current events, especially with the development of services that enable the live broadcasting of multimedia content, such as livestreams and livecasts[177]. As early as 2011, Yates and Paquette indicated that "social media is emerging as an important technology for disaster response"[178]. Today, the use of social media in crisis communication is rapidly expanding and spreading at an unprecedented pace[179].

Most importantly, studies indicate that individuals rely on social media in the absence of official information or when alternative information channels arise, providing supplementary details regarding ongoing crises[180]. Thus, as stated by London and Matthews, social media platforms are "increasingly seen as essential tools for communicating with affected communities who may be hard to reach during an emergency event"[181]. Yet, social media can be problematic during crises due to the rapid spread of misinformation, difficulties in controlling narratives, and the risk of misinterpretation. The lack of verification mechanisms may lead to the dissemination of false or misleading information, while public panic and emotional responses can amplify confusion. Additionally, organizations may struggle to maintain credibility if messages are inconsistent, delayed, or unclear. The growing speed of information also poses a significant challenge for crisis managers, who are required to update social media platforms in real-time during the

---

[176] A. Jungherr, "Twitter Use in Election Campaigns: A Systematic Literature Review", *Journal of Information Technology & Politics*, vol. 13, no. 1, 2016, pp. 72–91. DOI: https://doi.org/10.1080/19331681.2015.1132401

[177] B. Kosowski, A. Luzar A, *op. cit.*

[178] D. Yates, S. Paquette, "Emergency knowledge management and social media technologies: a case study of the 2010 Haitian earthquake", *International Journal of Information Management*, vol. 31, no. 1, 2011, pp. 6–13. DOI: https://doi.org/10.1016/j.ijinfomgt.2010.10.001

[179] M. Maal, M. Wilson-North, "Social media in crisis communication – the "do's" and "don'ts", *International Journal of Disaster Resilience in the Built Environment*, vol. 10, no. 5, 2019, pp. 379–391. DOI: https://doi.org/10.1108/IJDRBE-06-2014-0044

[180] T. Simon, A. Goldberg, B. Adini, "Socializing in emergencies—A review of the use of social media in emergency situations", *International Journal of Information Management*, v. 35, no. 5, 2015, pp. 609–619. DOI: https://doi.org/10.1016/j.ijinfomgt.2015.07.001

[181] J. Jr London, K. Matthews, *op. cit.*

event of a crisis. This fast-paced environment demands immediate response, creating pressure to maintain accuracy and consistency, while also managing the rapid influx of public inquiries and potential misinformation[182].

As Seeger explains, crisis communication is seen as the exchange of information between different stakeholders during times of significant uncertainty, when urgent action is needed, and important goals are at risk. This communication takes place through existing networks and channels, using different formats and styles of messaging. The key elements that influence the effectiveness of crisis communication include timely feedback, clarity and consistency of messages, tailoring information to different audiences, ensuring broad reach, and maintaining transparency, credibility, and coordination with relevant groups. As the author argues, communicating effectively in a crisis is essential—not just to organize response efforts and help people understand the complex situation, but also to support recovery, build resilience, and learn from the experience. Typically, communication evolves along with the crisis itself, starting with early warnings or risk signals before a crisis, and continuing through to rebuilding and reflection after the crisis ends[183].

One of the key principles of effective crisis communication, as pointed out by the US Centers for Disease Control and Prevention[184], is also the need for frequent, consistent, and empathetic messaging, which helps build credibility and maintain public trust. This aligns with the findings of Maal and Wilson-North, who also emphasize the importance of empathy and respect in fostering trust. They argue that honesty and transparency can help mitigate misinformation[185]. Additionally, factual accuracy and the credibility of content presented on social media are essential for maintaining public trust. They also stress the need for timely responses and consistent engagement before, during, and after crises. Moreover, in order to ensure public engagement and empowerment throughout a crisis, two-way communication, cultural awareness, alignment with official communication strategies,

---

182 M. Maal, M. Wilson-North, op. cit.

183 M. Seeger, *Crisis Communication*, Oxford Research Encyclopedia of Politics, 2022: https://oxfordre.com/politics/view/10.1093/acrefore/9780190228637.001.0001/acrefore-9780190228637-e-1537 [7.03.2025].

184 US Centers for Disease Control and Prevention, *Crisis and emergency risk communication (CERC) manual*, 2020. https://emergency.cdc.gov/cerc/manual/index.asp [7.03.2025].

185 M. Maal, M. Wilson-North, op. cit.

and providing actionable guidance are also described as essential. The same study identifies several key mistakes that organizations should avoid during crisis communication. The authors emphasize that speculation and personal opinions can damage credibility, and that posting offensive or inappropriate content may harm the organization's reputation. Additionally, they highlight the risks of ambiguous messaging, which can lead to misinterpretation. Relying on only one social media platform limits reach, while spelling errors can undermine professionalism. Finally, they argue that social media should be integrated into overall communication strategies, rather than treated as a separate initiative. For this reason, it is essential for city authorities and crisis management units to consider how social media should be utilized in the event of a disaster. The following chapter examines an example of the use of social media for communication with residents of the region during a flood situation.

Case study

Methodology

To analyze how city authorities used social media to communicate with residents during a crisis, the author employed a case study method. The study examines the case of communication of the mayor of Nysa, Kordian Kolbiarz, with the municipality's residents during a sudden flood in south-western Poland in September 2024 via the Facebook platform. The research focused on the mayor's official Facebook page (kordian.kolbiarz), specifically the announcements and comments posted on his profile between September 12 and September 18, 2024. The mayor's page has 14,000 followers[186], representing over 14% of the municipality's population.

The content analysis covered the period from the first mention of the flood threat on the mayor's Facebook page (September 12) and tracked the following days of escalating risk, the peak of the flood, and the eventual official withdrawal of the flood warning (September 18)a total of seven days. During this time, the mayor published 28 posts, many of them accompanied by images or labeled as "important announcement". These posts collectively received 4,303 reactions, 3,543 comments, and 5,343 shares.

[186] As of March 15, 2025.

The study was conducted in February 2025, and the author acknowledges that by this time, some crisis-period posts and comments may have been deleted. However, the research also took into account instances where the mayor edited posts in ways that significantly altered or supplemented the original message.

The study focused on:

1. The substantive content of the mayor's announcements, including the dates and times of publication.
2. The audience's comments, particularly recurring remarks regarding both the mayor's statements and the crisis situation.
3. The number of reactions, comments, and shares.

The case study provides a chronological analysis of the mayor's published messages, divided by day, supplemented by a brief description of key flood-related events essential for understanding the situation. These descriptions were reconstructed based on reports from local and national media. At this point, it should also be noted that the purpose of the analysis is not to reconstruct the full course of the flood or to examine its causes and consequences, but solely to focus on the messages that were communicated during that time.

The case study begins with a brief factual characterization of the Nysa municipality, including its hydrological features. The subsequent section analyzes the mayor's social media announcements directed at residents during the flood period.

About the Nysa Municipality

The Nysa Municipality (Gmina Nysa) is located in southwestern Poland, in the Opole Voivodeship, within the Nysa County (Powiat Nysa). It includes the town of Nysa and 26 villages (called in Polish "sołectwa" – the smallest administrative units in Poland). The municipality covers an area of approximately 217 km^2 and has a population of over 55,000 residents, with more than 40,000 living in Nysa itself.

Nysa is the third-largest city in the Opole Voivodeship. The Nysa Kłodzka River flows through the center of the municipality, and in 1971, an artificial retention reservoir—Lake Nyskie —was created on it. This reservoir is situated in close proximity to the town of Nysa. It covers an area of 2,075 hectares and has a total capacity of 122.1 million m^3, of which 55.8 million m^3 is designated as flood storage.

Lake Nyskie plays a crucial role in flood protection for areas located downstream. The dam forming the lake is a concrete-earth structure, extending over 5 km in length and reaching up to 14 meters in height. In addition to the Nysa Kłodzka River, several other rivers, including Płocha, Widna, and Biała Głuchołaska, also flow into the reservoir.

The Nysa Municipality is traversed not only by the Nysa Kłodzka River, but also by other rivers such as the Biała Głuchołaska, Ścinawa Niemodlińska, Kamienica, Cielnica, and Mora. The area of the Nysa Municipality is prone to periodic flooding primarily due to the presence of the Nysa Kłodzka River and its tributaries[187]. The hydrological characteristics of the region, including the mountainous course of the rivers, contribute to rapid and dynamic water surges. Particularly intense flooding events have been observed in the upper section of the Nysa Kłodzka and Biała Głuchołaska river basins, as well as in the area around Lake Nyskie. A historical analysis of floodwater levels shows that the highest values were recorded in the years: 1783, 1829, 1883, 1938, and 1997.

In July 1997, a flood caused the complete inundation of the Nysa Kłodzka River valley and the central areas of the town of Nysa. Despite the protective function of the Nyskie Lake reservoir, it was unable to stop the flood wave. A significant part of the town was submerged, and the water also affected surrounding villages (including Kubice, Konradowa, Wyszków Śląski, Biała Nyska, Morów, Iława, Przełęk, Hajduki Nyskie, and Lipowa). The disaster caused immense material damage, destroying residential infrastructure and workplaces. The flood led to building dampness, weakening of structures, as well as damage to foundations, roads, and the riverbed. Due to the scale of the destruction, the Nysa Municipality was one of the most affected areas in Poland during the so-called "flood of the millennium."

---

187 B. Szuba, „Problem zabezpieczenia przeciwpowodziowego miasta Nysy", *Technical Transactions/Czasopismo Techniczne. Architektura*, vol. 17, no. 108, 2011, pp. 253–257.

Analysis of crisis communication

Situational context

On Wednesday, September 11, a meteorological warning was issued for Nysa County by the Institute of Meteorology and Water Management (IMGW), forecasting heavy rainfall with a high probability of occurrence (90%)[188]. The announcement was released at 1:07 PM. The first signals of a potential flood for the region also came from the Czech Republic. On the same day, Czech authorities issued warnings about extreme rainfall. The Czech Minister of the Environment, Peter Hladík, stated at an emergency press conference that the situation could resemble the catastrophic floods of 1997[189]. Czech emergency services warned Polish authorities about the likelihood of a 100-year flood. Paweł Szymkowicz, mayor of Głuchołazy, a border town in Poland, noted in the media that "Czech forecasts paint a darker scenario than ours, but IMGW predictions also indicate water levels comparable to those of July 1997"[190].

September 12, Thursday

The first post by the mayor of Nysa regarding the flood threat appeared on his Facebook profile on September 12 at 7:55 AM. He informed the residents of the municipality about the flood risk due to continuous heavy rainfall. He also assured them that "the services responsible for the safety of our Municipality's residents are in constant contact and preparing for various developments in the situation." He appealed for caution and adherence to safety rules.

In his post, he included an infographic from the Government Security Center (Rządowe Centrum Bezpieczeństwa, RCB) with information on how to act in the event of a flood or inundation. This guide provided instructions on what to do before a flood, such as listening to threat warnings, ensuring that the family knows what to do during a flood, moving important documents and medications to higher floors, and charging your phone). The

---

188 Gmina Nysa, Komunikat meteo 105/2024: https://nysa.eu/ostrzezenia/komunikat-meteo-105-2024/ [10.03.2025].

189 TVN Meteo, *Czesi boją się powtórki z 1997 roku*, 2024: https://tvn24.pl/tvnmeteo/swiat/czesi-boja-sie-powtorki-z-1997-roku-st8082388 [10.03.2025].

190 K. Bińczyk, *„Wody jest więcej niż w 1997. Przygotujcie się". Czeskie służby ostrzegają Polaków, 2024*: https://wiadomosci.radiozet.pl/swiat/news-wody-jest-wiecej-niz-w-1997-przygotujcie-sie-czeskie-sluzby-ostrzegaja-polakow [10.03.2025].

guide also provided direction on what to do during a flood, such as preparing for evacuation (backpack icon), taking photos of the damage, not drinking water from wells, and disconnecting electricity and gas). The infographic also included the emergency number: 112.

This post received 46 reactions, 23 comments, and 27 shares. The comments included remarks that in 1997, people were also assured that nothing would happen, and reminders of the continuous lack of a flood relief channel in the municipality.

The second—and final—post of the day appeared at 3:55 PM. It stated that all spillway structures in the region were operational. The mayor, citing the National Water Authority (Wody Polskie), assured residents that "the water level in the Nysa reservoir is at a safe level, and there is no decision to increase water retention." At that time, the reservoir's fill level was 45.9 million m^3 of water, while its limit was 121.7 million m^3 (inflow: 14.97 m^3/s, outflow: 10 m^3/s). The response to this post was minimal (29 reactions, 10 comments).

September 13, Friday

On Friday, September 13, the levees between the villages of Przełęk and Biała Nyska began to seep. That day, three updates were posted on the mayor's profile at 12:44 PM, 2:58 PM, and 8:08 PM. The first post informed residents about the availability of sandbags. The mayor assured that "all services are active and monitoring the situation" and stated that "we are currently dealing with threats related to localized flooding."

In the second post, marked with an image labeled "Important Announcement," Kordian Kolbiarz informed residents about a 24-hour emergency hotline at the city hall, which they could contact in case of any "identified threats." In the comments, residents inquired about the water level of Lake Nysa and whether they should be concerned.

The final post, published late in the evening, reported that Territorial Defense Force soldiers were assisting in efforts to combat the flooding.

September 14, Saturday

A total of six posts were published on the mayor's profile on September 14. The first one appeared at 7:02 AM. The mayor shared "bad news" regarding the flood situation in local villages due to the Biała Głuchołaska River exceeding the alarm level. As he reported, flooding had already occurred in villages such as Morów, Hajduki Nyskie, and Siestrzechowice. Across the entire municipality "hundreds of local floods" had taken place. As he had informed, the Minister of Internal Affairs and Administration, Tomasz Siemoniak, arrived in the municipality, and a crisis management meeting was scheduled for 8:00 AM.

Shortly after, at 9:17 AM, the second post appeared on the mayor's profile, providing information that the reservoir was approximately 40% full (as of September 13, 6:00 PM) and that the planned water release was set at 250 m^3/s. He noted that the situation was constantly changing but assured residents that the emergency services were "continuously working to ensure our safety." In the comments, residents began reporting that their homes in Nysa were starting to flood.

At 10:14 AM, the mayor shared an announcement from the local waterworks AKWA, informing residents that reports of failures were being continuously received and appealing for responsible use of drinking water, as well as advising against discharging rainwater into the sanitary sewer system. The announcement assured residents that "there is no need to fear a shortage of tap water."

At 10:25 AM, another "important announcement" was published with phone duty schedules for municipal crisis management staff, providing a contact number "in case of identifying a threat." The post received 140 shares, but in the comments, several residents reported that the number was inactive ("no one is answering," "voicemail keeps turning on," "no response at all").

At 4:59 PM, the mayor shared another AKWA update stating that the water was safe to drink. As journalist Krzysztof Strauchmann reports, the information about the breached levees in Przełęk reached the district crisis management team in Nysa on Saturday around 6:00 PM (within the following 24 hours, the breach in the levee had expanded to a length of over 120 meters)[191].

The next and final post, however, was published at 8:17 PM, presenting the latest updates from the crisis management meeting attended by Polish Prime Minister Donald Tusk. The mayor informed the residents about the

191 K. Strauchmann, *Powódź 2024. Wielka woda zalała Nysę. Mieszkańcom na sesji rady miejskiej puściły nerwy*: https://nto.pl/powodz-2024-wielka-woda-zalala-nyse-mieszkancom-na-sesji-rady-miejskiej-puscily-nerwy/ar/c1-18867609 [10.03.2025].

increased water discharge from the lake to 400 m^3/s, as decided by the Polish Waters Management Board. He also made two assurances that later became the source of the greatest complaints from the residents:

1. The water continues to stay in the riverbed and is expected to stay there.
2. Our lake is almost half-empty, and it WILL CERTAINLY be able to prevent a potential flood.

In his post, Kordian Kolbiarz also emphasized that the greatest threat to Nysa comes from the Biała Głuchołaska River, local streams, brooks, creeks, and groundwater flooding. He reported that nearly all the villages and districts of Nysa were facing water surplus issues. He also appealed for calm, mutual assistance, and reliance on "verified and official sources of information."

This post triggered a flood of negative comments and reactions. Residents complained about being reassured that everything was under control, while the situation was unpredictable and constantly changing. However, the greatest number of complaints focused on the lack of a decision regarding water discharge from the lake when the first reports of heavy rainfall and potential flooding emerged. In the comments, residents began sharing photos of flooded properties and reporting the lack of assistance and access to sandbags.

September 15, Sunday

Late at night, at 1:08 AM on Sunday, the mayor of Nysa issued an urgent announcement on his social media account:

> *Based on the data and information we have just received; I am forced to declare a FLOOD ALERT FOR OUR ENTIRE MUNICIPALITY! Nearly the entire city and almost all of our villages are struggling with excessive water levels. State and local emergency services are engaged in protecting the health and lives of residents. A large number of citizens are defending their homes and apartments from flooding and destruction. (…) Unfortunately, the forecast for the coming hours is highly unfavorable, and we must be prepared for any scenario. This morning, at 8:00 AM, you will hear the sound of alarm sirens. This will confirm the implementation of the flood alert. Please make sure you are ready for an immediate evacuation from your current place of residence. There may be temporary power outages, so please ensure your mobile phones are fully charged. The situation is changing almost by every minute. I will keep you updated on everything. May God watch over us.*

The announcement was accompanied by the previously shared infographic from the RCB. In the comments, residents mainly asked where designated evacuation sites were and why the alert was issued so late. Others questioned how this message would reach elderly residents and how they were supposed to charge their phones when some districts were already without electricity. One commenter requested more specifics: "(...) We ask you to provide expected scenarios. Calling on God for help will not be of much use. We want to know what the plans are, the likelihood of the river Nysa Kłodzka overflowing, and if the bridges will be closed. (...)."

The next announcement appeared at 12:19 PM, more than eleven hours after the previous post, featuring a graphic with the words "Warning: Evacuation Recommended." The impatience and confusion of residents were evident in the comments, where they accused the mayor of failing to provide real-time updates. In his post, the mayor urged residents of several streets in Nysa to secure their belongings and "seek shelter outside these streets, in higher parts of the city." He also provided phone numbers where people could get information about available shelters. Additionally, he warned residents about the rising water levels in the Bielawski Canal, which posed a flooding risk to streets closer to the city center. He stated that the current water discharge from Lake Nyskie was at its "maximum" (600 m^3/s) and assured residents that "it would not be increased!" so the water should remain within the riverbanks. The post received 34 comments, in which many asked about the lake's current water levels.

Unfortunately, this message did not reflect the latest developments. At 10:35 AM, a dam breach occurred in Stronie Śląskie on the Morawka River. A massive surge of water flowed down the Biała Lądecka River into the Nysa Kłodzka basin, devastating numerous towns in the Lower Silesian Voivodeship, including Stronie Śląskie, Lądek-Zdrój, and Kłodzko. Officially, the Polish Water Authority confirmed the destruction of the dam more than two hours later (after 1:00 PM).

In response to the dam failure in Stronie Śląskie, at 1:39 PM, the mayor of Nysa posted a brief update titled "Breaking News." He announced that the water discharge from the lake had been increased from 600 m^3/s to 1000 m^3/s, and that bridges in town were being closed. His post sparked a wave of outrage from residents, who were frustrated by the mayor's earlier assurances that the lake's discharge rate would not be increased. People also demanded specific times for the bridge closures, as conflicting reports were circulating in the comments. Additionally, there were urgent pleas for public announcements to be made using loudspeakers, as many residents did not use Facebook or had already lost electricity.

Nearly an hour later, at 2:38 PM, another announcement was posted, informing parents that all childcare and educational institutions would be closed the following day. This post received only 20 comments, but all were negative, many filled with vulgar language. A significant number of commenters demanded the mayor's resignation from the office.

A short while later, at 3:17 PM, the fifth announcement of the day appeared:

> *SELF-EVACUATION!! Due to the increasing flood risk, I ask you to consider SELF-EVACUATION, meaning moving outside the danger zone. Residents of houses are urged to move to higher floors. In a moment, the alarm siren will sound – 'THE WATER IS COMING!'*

This post was later edited to include an additional message before the headline:

> *DEAR RESIDENTS! Unfortunately, we are unable to determine the strength and direction of the impending flood. Generally, it is safer 'across the river'! Let's pack documents (ID cards), keys, medication, a change of clothes for 48 hours, snacks, and water. You may take a blanket. A phone charger.*

The post sparked strong emotions. It received 563 comments, many written in panic and frustration, some containing vulgar language. Residents were outraged that such an important announcement was being made through the mayor's social media. Many commenters requested details about the danger zone and evacuation locations, especially given that bridges had already been closed, making it impossible to reach the area the mayor indicated as safer "across the river." Residents expressed confusion, not knowing where to go, how to evacuate, or what transportation options were available. They demanded concrete information, including medical points, open pharmacies, evacuation sites, and passable roads. Many criticized the previous assurances that the situation was under control, as well as the poor communication and organization:

- The way crisis communication is being handled shows a total lack of competence in City Hall.

- How can you wait until the last minute with such critical information? No details on where, what, or how! Evacuation should have been organized much earlier, before the bridges were closed. Now, how and where are people supposed to evacuate?

Due to the lack of official responses, residents began sharing information themselves, posting maps with safe routes and instructions on how to leave the city. Appeals for help evacuating families with children started appearing as "emergency services failed to assist for hours". One commenter, frustrated by the lack of clear answers, remarked that people should not have to scroll through comments just to get life-saving information in a crisis.

According to a regional newspaper, the high waters from the Biała Głuchołaska River reached downtown Nysa around 4:00 PM, approximately 45 minutes after the mayor's announcement. Through a network of old drainage canals, the water flooded several districts of the city, including the Nysa emergency medical unit[192].

The next and final post from the mayor came at 8:09 PM. It was addressed to "those still needing evacuation from flooded homes and apartments." The mayor mentioned that transportation was available to two buildings in the municipality and provided phone numbers for residents to "report their needs."

The comments under this post were filled with frustration, with many residents feeling abandoned. They pointed out that no vehicles with loudspeakers were driving through the city to spread messages. They reported issues with connectivity and signal loss, making it impossible to check online updates or request evacuation. Many were unsure how to reach the designated shelters due to the closed bridges. Calls to the numbers provided went unanswered for hours, leaving residents in desperate uncertainty.

September 16, Monday

On Monday, September 16, the first message appeared at 7:08 AM. It reported the water supply being cut off due to a damaged pipeline, as well as the maintained water discharge volume of 1000 m^3/s. Among the 195 comments, many residents requested specific information and asked for updates to be

---

192 K. Strauchmann, op. cit.

broadcast via loudspeakers in the city and surrounding villages. People were asking, "Where will drinking water be available and when?", "What is the action plan?", "Which roads can be used to leave Nysa?", "Can we return, or is another wave coming?". One comment read, "It's a disgrace that people have to rely on Facebook to figure out how to survive." However, no official responses were given to the comments.

The next post was published at 12:01 PM. The mayor urged residents to stay at home and informed them that "In a moment, we will hear sirens reminding us that the situation remains very serious." He also asked people to "get only information from reliable sources because, unfortunately, many people are spreading misinformation." This post received 276 responses, with many criticizing the lack of adequate and reliable updates from city officials, forcing residents to gather information on their own during the crisis. Commenters also pointed out how other municipalities were providing clear and precise updates, including evacuation locations with specific street details.

At 4:31 PM, the mayor published a post that generated 594 reactions, 382 comments, and was shared 1.9K times. In his message, Kordian Kolbiarz announced an official evacuation due to the high and sudden risk of the Nysa Kłodzka River levee failing. He urged residents to "evacuate as quickly as possible" and assured them that emergency services would soon arrive. He wrote, "(...) Make sure to evacuate to higher floors. The operation to save the levee is about to start, but we must be prepared for the worst. Let's stay together!" The post also featured a nearly 1.5-minute video repeating the same information. Comments were mainly filled with concerns that residents still did not know where and how to evacuate. Some expressed outrage over the mayor's earlier statements in national media, where he had assured the public that the situation was stable and there was no need to panic.

At 4:58 PM, the mayor posted a short update announcing a reduction in water discharge from the dam to 800 m^3/s to allow for a safe evacuation and repair of the weakened levee. The comments continued to contain requests for clear evacuation routes. Thirteen minutes later, at 5:11 PM, another message was posted, reaffirming that the evacuation order remained in effect and that the water discharge from the lake would be reduced from 6:00 PM onward. Residents kept asking for loudspeaker announcements and clear guidance on where and how to evacuate.

According to a regional journalist, a military commander deemed it too dangerous to send soldiers onto the embankments due to the high-water level. Authorities planned to use helicopters to drop bags of stones into the breaches. Meanwhile, residents, mobilizing through the internet and phone calls, spontaneously rushed to help reinforce the levees. At the same time, the crisis team delivered tons of sand and crushed stone to the site, along with equipment, lighting, firefighters, and military personnel[193].

September 17, Tuesday

The next post was published on Tuesday at 2:25 AM. The mayor thanked the residents for their fight for Nysa, acknowledging those who had stepped up to reinforce the levee. He included a photo of media headlines referring to the "heroic struggle of residents for the levee." In the comments, some people pushed back against the mayor's use of the word "we." They pointed out that it had been a small group of residents who had mobilized people to help and take action, despite regulations prohibiting entry onto the levee:

> *(...) We moved thousands of sandbags weighing tons, wading through mud, sometimes just a meter away from the raging river. We risked our lives—if someone had slipped, we wouldn't have been able to save them. If the levee had failed, the hundreds, or at the peak moment possibly over a thousand residents, could have lost their lives!*

However, some commenters defend the mayor, posting photos to show that he, too, worked on the levee. Another post appeared again during the night, at 3:22 AM. It was a request for assistance in delivering transport straps. In the comments, people offered help, but there was still significant criticism of the mayor's actions and ongoing questions about the level of risk.

The next post on Tuesday was published at 9:43 AM. The mayor stated that "everything indicates that Nysa has been saved." He thanked residents for their involvement in protecting the levee and announced a planned reduction in the water release to 600 m^3/s. He also noted that some risky weak points on the levee were still being managed by emergency services. The post received 1,000 reactions and 335 comments. Many residents congratulated and thanked each other. Some, however, sought to assign blame, accusing the mayor and his team of failing to take proper action

[193] Ibidem.

when alarming weather forecasts were first issued. Others stated that Nysa was saved thanks to "civil disobedience" and questioned who would have taken responsibility if the levee had broken and hundreds of people had been swept away by the floodwaters.

At 3:26 PM, the mayor published a post debunking rumors claiming that "the dam has collapsed, that water has been released from the reservoir into the flood relief channel, and that other disasters have occurred." He clarified that the water appearing in one of the city's districts was the result of floodwaters moving from other areas of the municipality. In the comments, people appealed for help from villagers in the Nysa municipality who were still struggling with floodwater.

The last post of the day appeared at 9:05 PM. The mayor announced that at midnight, the evacuation order for Nysa would be lifted (although it would remain in effect for certain streets). The following day at 8:00 AM, this would be confirmed by alarm sirens. He urged residents to remain cautious, as the flood warning was still active. In the comments, residents mainly criticized the ineffective alarm systems, writing that in some areas, they were not audible and that the lack of megaphone announcements about the evacuation had caused confusion.

A follow-up to this post appeared the next day at 8:22 AM. The mayor clarified that instead of siren signals canceling the evacuation, voice announcements had been chosen. Comments indicated that some residents did not understand what the different signals meant, while others only heard scattered, isolated words, which further fueled panic.

Analysis of communication – advantages and disadvantages of using social media for crisis communication

The above analysis enabled the author to identify the strengths and weaknesses of using social media for communication with residents during a crisis, as well as to highlight key elements that should be taken into account by local authorities when using this communication channel. In order to develop universal guidelines, the author collected feedback from followers in the comments and drew conclusions based on the mayor's official communications.

Weaknesses in communication

As summarized by journalist Krzysztof Strauchmann:

> *Poor communication with residents was a weak point during the recent flood operation. In Nysa, residents lacked clear and precise information on what to do, where and how to evacuate, and where buses would be arriving. They didn't know which areas would be threatened by water and which would be safe, or which routes were safe to leave the city. The initial messages were distinctly reassuring, claiming the situation was under control. When things became more dangerous, some people did not believe the warnings and downplayed the threat. Buses sent to evacuate people often returned with empty seats.*[194]

The journalist also pointed out that an unknown number of users on this social media platform had previously been blocked by the mayor and even by the city's official profile. As a result, they were unable to see these critical messages.

In a later interview, the mayor himself admitted that "*our information system was not optimal, it wasn't the best, it didn't reach everyone,*" and that "*the communication chaos was enormous.*" He also stated that he did not engage in discussions with commenters, as there was no time for it[195].

An analysis of the mayor's communication during the crisis reveals several major shortcomings that negatively affected residents' sense of security. The lack of early warnings, imprecise and infrequent updates, and one-way communication based primarily on Facebook contributed to growing frustration, fear, and distrust toward local authorities. Obtaining verified information from the account of a person directly representing the city was clearly important to residents. However, the mayor and his team, preoccupied with managing the crisis, failed to assign a dedicated person who could provide residents with crucial safety information in a dynamic and challenging situation. This intensified the sense of chaos and lack of support from the authorities. A detailed analysis of the weak points in the mayor's communication with residents during the crisis is presented in Table 1.

---

[194] Ibidem.

[195] D. Klimczak, *Nasz system informacji nie był optymalny - Kordian Kolbiarz o działaniach władz miasta w czasie powodzi (02.10.2024):* https://radio.opole.pl/124,10361,nasz-system-informacji-nie-byl-optymalny-kordian

Table 1: Weaknesses in the mayor of Nysa's Communication During the Flood

Problem Area	Description of the Issue	Consequences
Delayed response to the crisis and inconsistent messaging	No early warning about the approaching threat. Initial reassurances that the situation was under control were followed by a sudden evacuation order. Early statements downplaying the risk turned out to be inaccurate.	- Residents had no time to prepare for the flood. - A sense of chaos and misinformation. - Loss of trust in local authorities. - The threat was not taken seriously by many.
Lack of detail in official statements	The mayor communicated only general information. Evacuation and self-evacuation messages lacked specifics. Residents reported not knowing where the safe zones were, how to evacuate, or which roads were passable.	- Residents felt anxious and frustrated. - Increased sense of uncertainty. - People searched for information on their own, which led to misinformation.
Infrequent updates	Hours passed between updates despite the rapidly changing situation. Residents pleaded for news in the comment sections.	- Residents were left alone at night with no guidance. - No sense that the situation was being properly managed.
Lack of multi-channel communication	The mayor used only Facebook to communicate, although not all residents had internet access or used the platform. Citizens complained about the absence of announcements via loudspeakers, radio signals, or other offline channels. The flood warning and evacuation notices were mostly posted on Facebook, which received heavy criticism.	- Elderly individuals and those not using social media may not have received critical information. - Information chaos.
Lack of a clear communication strategy	The messages were chaotic, irregular, lacked structure and prioritized. No indication was given about where to find reliable information.	- Disorganized information flow. - Residents had to search for updates on their own. - A feeling of being abandoned by authorities.

Problem Area	Description of the Issue	Consequences
Lack of interaction with residents	Comments contained specific questions and calls for help, but the mayor's team did not respond. Many questions remained unanswered.	– A sense that authorities were ignoring citizens' concerns. – Growing frustration and social tension.
Lack of transparency in actions	No detailed information about the activities of the crisis management team or regular status updates.	– Rising mistrust in local authorities. – Speculation and rumors on social media. – Perception that the mayor "was not doing anything."

Source: Author's own compilation.

The above analysis enabled the formulation of recommendations regarding key elements that should be taken into account when planning a city's communication strategy during a crisis, specifically when using social media. These include:

- Preparation of pre-defined communication scenarios for crisis situations – establishing procedures and message templates in advance that can be quickly adapted to the situation. These should include, among others, guidelines on how to behave during a crisis (as well as how to prepare for one), evacuation methods, and reliable sources of information.
- Early warning of residents using pre-prepared crisis materials – developing procedures that enable the immediate publication of initial messages as soon as the risk of flooding or another crisis arises.
- Avoiding reassurances in risk situations – refraining from offering assurances that may later prove inaccurate or misleading.
- Appointing a dedicated crisis spokesperson – designating a spokesperson or a crisis communication team. This person/team would be responsible for regularly updating the mayor's profile (or a dedicated account) and responding to residents' questions in real time.
- Including critical and specific information in social media posts – providing more detailed instructions, such as evacuation routes, shelter locations, and key information points.
- Frequent updates – establishing the frequency of social media posts as part of the communication strategy, especially during rapidly evolving crises.

- Informing residents about alternative communication channels – Providing information on where and how residents can access city updates outside of social media platforms.
- Rapid response to misinformation – monitoring for false information and immediately correcting it through official communication channels.

The development of a strategy for the use of social media in crisis situations should take into account both the advantages and disadvantages of these platforms. As demonstrated by the analyzed case, on the one hand, social media (in this case, Facebook) are platforms where people actively seek real-time information during a crisis. Their inclusion in a city's crisis communication strategy would not only meet the needs of residents but would also reflect a response aligned with global communication trends.

Among the observed advantages of using social media during a crisis are primarily the ability to publish urgent messages instantly and reach a wide audience — especially thanks to the sharing functionality. They also allow for greater transparency, as feedback in the form of comments can help assess the clarity and effectiveness of the published content or highlight overlooked issues from the residents' point of view. Social media are widely accessible, user-friendly, and allow for the rapid sharing of multimedia content — which can significantly support the work of communication teams during an emergency.

Unfortunately, as such posts can be created quickly, they may also be published impulsively or based on inaccurate data. Therefore, it is crucial to include a verification team in the communication process to check the accuracy of the shared information. It should also be kept in mind that technical failures or unpredictable events may prevent users from accessing social media and, consequently, vital updates. These individuals must be continuously informed of alternative offline sources where they can obtain key information.

One of the biggest drawbacks of social media platforms is the lack of control city authorities have over them. The algorithms and the way content is distributed are completely independent of the governing bodies, which means the reach of important posts may be limited. Critical information about evacuation or available aid might not reach all residents or may appear in a different order than originally intended, which can further intensify the sense of chaos and misinformation.

Conclusions

The case study analysis made it possible to answer the research questions posed. Firstly, individuals expect timely, clear, and detailed information, including early warnings, evacuation procedures, safe zones, road accessibility, and reliable sources of updates. Transparency and honesty are crucial — people value sincere communication over empty reassurances, especially when the situation is uncertain and evolving. They want to see that city authorities are present, engaged, and actively working to ensure the safety of residents.

Secondly, effective crisis communication should involve pre-prepared communication scenarios, a designated crisis spokesperson, frequent updates, specific instructions relevant to residents, and active engagement with the audience. It is essential to ensure transparency, consistency, and availability of alternative communication channels beyond social media.

Finally, using social media for communication purposes during a crisis has both advantages and disadvantages. On the one hand, it allows for rapid information dissemination, direct engagement with residents, and the ability to quickly update messages as the situation evolves. On the other hand, it can exclude individuals without access to the internet or specific platforms, increase the spread of misinformation, and, if not managed properly, lead to confusion and a lack of trust — especially when updates are infrequent, vague, or fail to respond to residents' concerns.

Social media are playing an increasingly vital role in crisis communication. Nevertheless, they should not be treated as the primary — let alone the sole — source of communication due to the various limitations these platforms present. For this reason, cities should develop a well-structured crisis communication strategy that incorporates social media while considering both the strengths and weaknesses of this communication channel.

References

BIŃCZYK, K., *„Wody jest więcej niż w 1997. Przygotujcie się". Czeskie służby ostrzegają Polaków, 2024*. https://wiadomosci.radiozet.pl/swiat/news-wody-jest-wiecej-niz-w-1997-przygotujcie-sie-czeskie-sluzby-ostrzegaja-polakow [10.03.2025].

COOMBS, W. T., "Protecting organization reputations during a crisis: The development and application of situational crisis communication theory", *Corporate Reputation Review*, vol. 10, no. 3, 2007, pp. 163–176. DOI: https://doi.org/10.1057/palgrave.crr.1550049

GMINA NYSA, *Komunikat meteo 105/2024*. https://nysa.eu/ostrzezenia/komunikat-meteo-105-2024/ [10.03.2025].

JUNGHERR, A., "Twitter Use in Election Campaigns: A Systematic Literature Review", *Journal of Information Technology & Politics*, vol. 13, no. 1, 2016, pp. 72–91. DOI: https://doi.org/10.1080/19331681.2015.1132401

KLIMCZAK, D., *Nasz system informacji nie był optymalny" - Kordian Kolbiarz o działaniach władz miasta w czasie powodzi (02.10.2024)*: https://radio.opole.pl/124,10361,nasz-system-informacji-nie-byl-optymalny-kordian [10.03.2025].

KOSOWSKI, B., *Komunikacja ze społeczeństwem w zarządzaniu sytuacjami kryzysowymi*, in: *Państwo, gospodarka, społeczeństwo w integrującej się Europie*, edited by Klemens Budzowski, Krakowskie Towarzystwo Edukacyjne, Kraków 2003, pp. 191–202.

KOSOWSKI, B., LUZAR A., *Potencjał wykorzystania mediów społecznościowych w sytuacjach kryzysowych - zarys problemu*, in: *Prasa lokalna i samorządowa: propozycje zmian legislacyjnych*, edited by A. Gołębiowska, P. B. Zientarski, Szkoła Główna Służby Pożarniczej, Warszawa 2020, pp. 125–136.

LONDON, J. Jr, MATTHEWS, K., "Crisis communication on social media - lessons from Covid-19", *Journal of Decision Systems*, vol. 31, no. 1–2, 2021, pp. 150–170. DOI: https://doi.org/10.1080/12460125.2021.1926612

MAAL, M., WILSON-NORTH, M., "Social media in crisis communication – the "do's" and "don'ts", *International Journal of Disaster Resilience in the Built Environment*, vol. 10, no. 5, 2019, pp. 379–391. DOI: https://doi.org/10.1108/IJDRBE-06-2014-0044

SEEGER, M., Crisis Communication, *Oxford Research Encyclopedia of Politics, 2022*: https://oxfordre.com/politics/view/10.1093/acrefore/9780190228637.001.0001/acrefore-9780190228637-e-1537 [7.03.2025].

SIMON, T., GOLDBERG, A., ADINI, B., “Socializing in emergencies—A review of the use of social media in emergency situations”, *International Journal of Information Management*, vol. 35, no. 5, 2015, pp. 609–619. DOI: https://doi.org/10.1016/j.ijinfomgt.2015.07.001.

STRAUCHMANN, K., *Powódź 2024. Wielka woda zalała Nysę. Mieszkańcom na sesji rady miejskiej puściły nerwy*: https://nto.pl/powodz-2024-wielka-woda-zalala-nyse-mieszkancom-na-sesji-rady-miejskiej-puscily-nerwy/ar/c1-18867609 [10.03.2025].

SUTTON, J., GIBSON, C. B.; SPIRO, E. S., LEAGUE, C.. FITZHUGH, S. M.; BUTTS, C. T., “What it takes to get passed on: Message content, style, and structure as predictors of retransmission in the Boston marathon bombing response”, *PLoS ONE*, vol. 10, no. 8: e0134452, 2015. DOI: https://doi.org/10.1371/journal.pone.0134452

SZUBA, B., „Problem zabezpieczenia przeciwpowodziowego miasta Nysy”, *Technical Transactions/Czasopismo Techniczne. Architektura*, vol. 17, no. 108, 2011, pp. 253–257.

TVN METEO, *Czesi boją się powtórki z 1997 roku, 2024*. https://tvn24.pl/tvnmeteo/swiat/czesi-boja-sie-powtorki-z-1997-roku-st8082388 [10.03.2025].

US CENTERS FOR DISEASE CONTROL AND PREVENTION, *Crisis and emergency risk communication (CERC) manual*, 2020. https://emergency.cdc.gov/cerc/manual/index.asp [7.03.2025].

YATES, D.; PAQUETTE, S., “Emergency knowledge management and social media technologies: a case study of the 2010 Haitian earthquake”, *International Journal of Information Management*, vol. 31, no. 1, 2011, pp. 6–13. DOI: https://doi.org/10.1016/j.ijinfomgt.2010.10.001

Studies in Politics, Security and Society

Edited by Stanisław Sulowski

Vol. 1 Robert Wiszniowski (ed.): Challenges to Representative Democracy. A European Perspective. 2015.

Vol. 2 Jarosław Szymanek: Theory of Political Representation. 2015.

Vol. 3 Alojzy Z. Nowak (ed.): Global Financial Turbulence in the Euro Area. Polish Perspective. 2015.

Vol. 4 Jolanta Itrich-Drabarek: The Civil Service in Poland. Theory and Experience. 2015.

Vol. 5 Agnieszka Rothert: Power of Imagination. Education, Innovations and Democracy. 2016.

Vol. 6 Zbysław Dobrowolski: Combating Corruption and Other Organizational Pathologies. 2017.

Vol. 7 Vito Breda: The Objectivity of Judicial Decisions. A Comparative Analysis of Nine Jurisdictions. 2017.

Vol. 8 Anna Sroka: Accountability and democracy in Poland and Spain. 2017.

Vol. 9 Anna Sroka / Fanny Castro-Rial Garrone / Rubén Darío Torres Kumbrián (eds.): Radicalism and Terrorism in the 21st Century. Implications for Security. 2017.

Vol. 10 Filip Pierzchalski: Political Leadership in Morphogenetic Perspective. 2017.

Vol. 11 Alina Petra Marinescu: The Discursive Dimension of Employee Engagement and Disengagement. Accounts of keeping and leaving jobs in present-day Bucharest organizations. 2017.

Vol. 12 Jacek Giedrojć: Competition, Coordination, Social Order. Responsible Business, Civil Society, and Government in an Open Society. 2017.

Vol. 13 Filip Ilkowski: Capitalist Imperialism in Contemporary Theoretical Frameworks. 2017.

Vol. 14 Leszek Leszczyński / Adam Szot (eds.): Discretionary Power of Public Admin istration. Its Scope and Control. 2017.

Vol. 15 Tadeusz Klementewicz: Understanding Politics. Theory, Procedures, Narratives. 2017.

Vol. 16 Tomasz Bichta: Political Systems of the Former Yugoslavia. 2018

Vol. 17 Miroslav Palárik / Alena Mikulášová / Martin Hetényi / Róbert Arpáš: The City and Region Against the Backdrop of Totalitarianism. 2018

Vol. 18 Jolanta Itrich-Drabarek / Stanisław Mazur / Justyna Wiśniewska-Grzelak (eds.): The Transformations of the Civil Service in Poland in Comparison with International Experience. 2018.

Vol. 19 Jerzy Juchnowski / R. Jan Sielezin / Ewa Maj: The Image of "White" and "Red" Russia in the Polish Political Thought of the 19th and 20th Century. Analogies and Parallels. 2018.

Vol. 20 Roman Kuźniar: Europe in the International Order. 2018.

Vol. 21 Piotr Jaroszyński: Europe - the Clash of Civilisations. 2018.

Vol. 22 Stanisław Filipowicz: Truth and the Will to Illusion. 2018.

Vol. 23 Andrzej Szeptycki: Contemporary Relations between Poland and Ukraine. The "Strategic Partnership" and the Limits Thereof. 2019.

Vol. 24 Sylwester Gardocki / Rafał Ożarowski / Rafał Ulatowski (eds.): The Islamic World in International Relations. 2019.

Vol. 25 Jacek Zaleśny (ed.): Constitutional Courts in Post-Soviet States. Between the Model of a State of Law and Its Local Application. 2019.

Vol. 26 Andrzej Antoszewski / Przemysław Żukiewicz / Mateusz Zieliński / Katarzyna. Domagała: Formation of Government Coalition in Westminster Democracies. Towards a Network Approach. 2020.

Vol. 27 Joanna Osiejewicz: Global Governance of Oil and Gas Resources in the International Legal Perspective. 2020.

Vol. 28 Anita Oberda-Monkiewicz: Poland-Mexico towards a Strategic Partnership. 2020.

Vol. 29 Bartosz Czepil / Wojciech Opioła: Ethnic diversity and local governance quality. The case of Opole Province in Poland. 2020.

Vol. 30 Adam Szymański / Jakub Wódka / Wojciech Ufel / Amanda Dziubińska: Between Fair and Rigged. Elections as a Key Determinant of the 'Borderline Political Regime' - Turkey in Comparative Perspective. 2020.

Vol. 31 Tomasz Grzegorz Grosse (ed.): Fuel for Dominance. On the Economic Bases of Geopolitical Supremacy. 2020.

Vol. 32 Dariusz Jarosz / Maria Pasztor: From Subjection to Independence. Post-World War II Polish-Italian Relations. 2020.

Vol. 33 Paweł Sekuła: Chernobyl Liquidators. The Unknown Story. With the Testimony of the President of Latvia. 2020.

Vol. 34 Kamil Glinka (ed.): Urban Policy System in Strategic Perspective: From V4 to Ukraine. 2020.

Vol. 35 Paweł Lesiński: At the Origins of German Liberalism: the State in the Thought of Robert von Mohl. 2020.

Vol. 36 Jana Popovicsová (ed.): Reflexions about a Cultural and Social Phenomenon: Identity. 2020.

Vol. 37 Agnes Bernek: Geopolitics of Central and Eastern Europe in the 21st Century. From the Buffer Zone to the Gateway Zone. 2021.

Vol. 38 Marek Antoni Musioł: The European Union as a Post-Lisbon Regional Security Complex. 2021.

Vol. 39 Alina Petra Marinescu: Manipulation in the Disclosure of the Securitate Files. The Case of Mona Muscă. 2021

Vol. 40 Jiří Zákravský: Cycling Diplomacy. Undemocratic Regimes and Professional Road Cycling Teams Sponsorship. 2021.

Vol. 41 Mirosław Karwat / Filip Pierzchalski / Marcin Tobiasz (eds.): Constituents of Political Theory. Selected Articles of the Warsaw School of Political Theory. 2021.

Vol. 42 Angieszka Bieńczyk-Missala: Preventing Mass Human-Rights Violations and Atrocity Crimes. 2021.

Vol. 43 Jan Garlicki: Political Participation Capital. 2021.

Vol. 44 Mirosław Karwat: Theory of Provocation. In Light of Political Science. 2022.

Vol. 45 Anna Sroka / Piotr Potejko / Rubén Darío Torres Kumbrián (eds.): Migration and Border Security. Global Perspectives. 2021.

Vol. 46 Stanisław Sulowski / Tomasz Słomka (eds.): The Political System of Poland. Tradition and Contemporaneity. 2022.

Vol. 47 Ewelina Kancik-Kołtun / Josef Smolík (eds.): New Political Parties in the Party Systems of the Czech Republic. 2022.

Vol. 48 Ewa Feder-Sempach: Economic Populism in British and American Political Discourse. A Comparative Analysis of Boris Johnson's and Donald Trump's Speeches. 2022.

Vol. 49 Katarzyna Kołodziejczyk (ed.): The EU Towards the Global South During the COVID-19 Pandemic. 2022.

Vol. 50 Silvia Amato: Public Undertakings of Nuclear Waste Storage. The Role of the Government in the Dissemination of Public Knowledge. 2022.

Vol. 51 Agnieszka Cholewińska-Nielsen: Evolving Humanitarianism. The Work of the International Red Cross and Red Crescent Movement. 2022.

Vol. 52 Josef Smolik / Ewelina Kancik-Kołtun: New Political Parties in the Party System of Poland. 2023.

Vol. 53 Rafał Wiśniewski / Elżbieta Szyszlak / Radosław Zenderowski (eds.): Cultural Security. Theory – Selected Aspects – Case Studies. 2023.

Vol. 54 Filip Pierzchalski: Political Leadership: Structure – Consciousness – Emotions. 2023.

Vol. 55 Łukasz Zamęcki / Li-Jiuan Chen-Rabich (eds.): The Democratisation Process of Poland and Taiwan: Comparative Perspective. 2023.

Vol. 56 Marcin Gajek: Refusing to be Forgotten: Southern Conservatism and the Political Thought of M. E. Bradford. 2023.

Vol. 57 Sulowski Stanisław (ed.): Security Challenges at the Dawn of a New International Order. 2023.

Vol. 58 Alicja Z. Nowak / Kinga Anna Gajda (eds.): University and War in Ukraine. 2023.

Vol. 59 Bernard Wiśniewski / Paulina Polko (eds.): Contemporary Understanding of Security and Its Contexts. 2024.

Vol. 60 Aleksander Żołnierski / Dariusz Jaruga (eds.): Big Data. Post-truth and Disinformation in Politics and Economy during Times of Conflict. 2024.

Vol. 61 Mirosław Karwat / Marcin Tobiasz / Jacek Ziółkowski (eds.): Constituents of Political Theory (2). Selected Articles by the Warsaw School of Political Theory. 2025.

Vol. 62 Katarzyna Stachurska-Szczesiak: Sustainable Development. Theoretical Approach. 2025.

Vol. 63 Joanna Sanecka-Tyczyńska: Reason of State in Contemporary Polish Political Thought. 2025.

Vol. 64 Agnieszka Kampka / Wojciech Mincewicz (eds.): A Worrying Present and an Uncertain Future. Challenges for Security in Central and Eastern Europe Region. 2025.

Vol. 65 Robert Geisler and Tomasz Pawłuszko (eds.): Public Policy and Local Crises. Lessons from Poland and Central Europe. 2025.

Vol. 47 Ewelina Kancik-Kołtun / Josef Smolík (eds.): New Political Parties in the Party Systems of the Czech Republic. 2022.

Vol. 48 Ewa Feder-Sempach: Economic Populism in British and American Political Discourse. A Comparative Analysis of Boris Johnson's and Donald Trump's Speeches. 2022.

Vol. 49 Katarzyna Kołodziejczyk (ed.): The EU Towards the Global South During the COVID-19 Pandemic. 2022.

Vol. 50 Silvia Amato: Public Undertakings of Nuclear Waste Storage. The Role of the Government in the Dissemination of Public Knowledge. 2022.

Vol. 51 Agnieszka Cholewińska-Nielsen: Evolving Humanitarianism. The Work of the International Red Cross and Red Crescent Movement. 2022.

Vol. 52 Josef Smolik / Ewelina Kancik-Kołtun: New Political Parties in the Party System of Poland. 2023.

Vol. 53 Rafał Wiśniewski / Elżbieta Szyszlak / Radosław Zenderowski (eds.): Cultural Security. Theory – Selected Aspects – Case Studies. 2023.

Vol. 54 Filip Pierzchalski: Political Leadership: Structure – Consciousness – Emotions. 2023.

Vol. 55 Łukasz Zamęcki / Li-Jiuan Chen-Rabich (eds.): The Democratisation Process of Poland and Taiwan: Comparative Perspective. 2023.

Vol. 56 Marcin Gajek: Refusing to be Forgotten: Southern Conservatism and the Political Thought of M. E. Bradford. 2023.

Vol. 57 Sulowski Stanisław (ed.): Security Challenges at the Dawn of a New International Order. 2023.

Vol. 58 Alicja Z. Nowak / Kinga Anna Gajda (eds.): University and War in Ukraine. 2023.

Vol. 59 Bernard Wiśniewski / Paulina Polko (eds.): Contemporary Understanding of Security and Its Contexts. 2024.

Vol. 60 Aleksander Żołnierski / Dariusz Jaruga (eds.): Big Data. Post-truth and Disinformation in Politics and Economy during Times of Conflict. 2024.

Vol. 61 Mirosław Karwat / Marcin Tobiasz / Jacek Ziółkowski (eds.): Constituents of Political Theory (2). Selected Articles by the Warsaw School of Political Theory. 2025.

Vol. 62 Katarzyna Stachurska-Szczesiak: Sustainable Development. Theoretical Approach. 2025.

Vol. 63 Joanna Sanecka-Tyczyńska: Reason of State in Contemporary Polish Political Thought. 2025.

Vol. 64 Agnieszka Kampka / Wojciech Mincewicz (eds.): A Worrying Present and an Uncertain Future. Challenges for Security in Central and Eastern Europe Region. 2025.

Vol. 65 Robert Geisler and Tomasz Pawłuszko (eds.): Public Policy and Local Crises. Lessons from Poland and Central Europe. 2025.

www.peterlang.com